Cambridge Elements

Elements in Applied Social Psychology
edited by
Susan Clayton
College of Wooster, Ohio

HATE SPEECH

Janet B. Ruscher
Tulane University

CAMBRIDGE
UNIVERSITY PRESS

Shaftesbury Road, Cambridge CB2 8EA, United Kingdom

One Liberty Plaza, 20th Floor, New York, NY 10006, USA

477 Williamstown Road, Port Melbourne, VIC 3207, Australia

314–321, 3rd Floor, Plot 3, Splendor Forum, Jasola District Centre,
New Delhi – 110025, India

103 Penang Road, #05–06/07, Visioncrest Commercial, Singapore 238467

Cambridge University Press is part of Cambridge University Press & Assessment,
a department of the University of Cambridge.

We share the University's mission to contribute to society through the pursuit of
education, learning and research at the highest international levels of excellence.

www.cambridge.org
Information on this title: www.cambridge.org/9781009534673

DOI: 10.1017/9781009534666

When citing this work, please include a reference to the DOI 10.1017/9781009534666

First published 2024

A catalogue record for this publication is available from the British Library

ISBN 978-1-009-53467-3 Hardback
ISBN 978-1-009-53468-0 Paperback
ISSN 2631-777X (online)
ISSN 2631-7761 (print)

Hate Speech

Elements in Applied Social Psychology

DOI: 10.1017/9781009534666
First published online: November 2024

Janet B. Ruscher
Tulane University

Author for correspondence: Janet B. Ruscher, ruscher@tulane.edu

Abstract: Hate speech comprises any form of hateful or contemptuous expression that attacks, degrades, or vilifies people based on their social identities. This Element focuses on hate speech targeting social identities that are devalued by a society's dominant groups, and that is likely to evoke, promote, or legitimize harms such violence, discrimination, and oppression. After detailing the ways in which hate speech is expressed (e.g., through derogatory labels, metaphors, offensive imagery), the production of hate speech is explored at the individual level (e.g., prejudiced attitudes), group level (e.g., realistic intergroup threat), and societal level (e.g., hierarchy maintenance; free speech protections). A discussion of the effects of blatant and anonymous hate speech on targets (e.g., anxiety and depression) and nontargets (e.g., stereotype activation; desensitization; fomenting violence) follows. Finally, the effectiveness of mitigation efforts is explored, including use of computer-based technologies, speech codes, confrontation, and counterspeech.

Keywords: hate speech, racist language, prejudice, systemic racism, racism

ISBNs: 9781009534673 (HB), 9781009534680 (PB), 9781009534666 (OC)
ISSNs: 2631-777X (online), 2631-7761 (print)

Contents

1 Introductory Ideas   1

2 Forms of Hate Speech   6

3 Factors Contributing to Hate Speech   16

4 Consequences of Hate Speech   30

5 Mitigation Efforts   41

6 Conclusion   51

   References   54

Students admitted to an Ivy League university circulate obscene racist and anti-Semitic memes. The university rescinds their offers of admission.

(Kamenetz et al., 2017)

A television personality asserts that an "endless chain of migrant caravans" make America "poorer, and dirtier, and more divided."

(Moran, 2018)

Finnish politicians are charged with criminal hate speech for anti-Muslim internet postings.

(Pettersson, 2019)

A police chief is fired after a recording of his use of numerous racial expletives is made public.

(Valencia, 2022)

An African American election worker reports being told "you should be glad it's 2020 and not 1920. You should hang with your mother for treason."
(Select Committee to Investigate the January 6th Attack on the US Capitol, 2022)

1 Introductory Ideas

During the past fifty years, scholars interested in prejudiced communication have focused heavily on subtle, covert, or indirect modes of prejudice expression (Cervone, Augoustinos, & Maass, 2021; Forscher et al., 2015). More recently, however, there has been an explosion of scholarly interest in prejudiced communication that is explicitly derogatory, incendiary, and hateful. This shifting interest is evident in the dramatic increase of scholarly publications about hate speech indexed in the Web of Science database over the past ten years, seeing a sevenfold increase overall from the period 2013–2017 to the period 2018–2022 (annual Ms = 39.2 and 279.6, respectively), which includes a tenfold increase within psychology and communication (annual Ms = 10.6 and 121.4, respectively). Article topics tend to cluster around basic hate speech issues (e.g., free speech; racism), specific target groups or medium used (e.g., anti-LGBTQA+; cyberbullying), and the detection of hate speech through computerized strategies (Tontodimamma et al., 2021). Perhaps the digital era has rendered hate speech more observable than in previous decades: The "citizen journalist" captures cell phone video, social media platforms provide outlets for viral communication, and the 24-hour news cycle shares otherwise obscure public comments across global outlets. Given that being targeted by hate speech on the basis of race, gender, or sexual minority status is extremely common (e.g., Ellingworth et al., 2023; Nielsen, 2002; Pew Research Center, 2013), it also is possible that the incidence of hate speech objectively has increased in recent decades; an increase certainly is feasible, given the rise of radical right-wing populism in industrialized nations

(Cervone, Augoustinos, & Maass, 2021), populist rhetoric that dehumanizes and promotes violence against ethnic minority cultures (Wahlström, Törnberg, & Ekbrand, 2020), and the erosion of norms against using overtly derogatory language (Bilewicz & Soral, 2020). Or perhaps a little both: Hate speech may have both increased in prevalence and also become increasingly more public. Whatever the underlying reason, the contemporary omnipresence of hate speech is evident. But what forms does it take, what motivates and perpetuates its expression, what effects does hate speech have on targets, nontargets, and society, and what strategies can combat or mitigate it?

A working definition of hate speech and the Element's focus are introduced, followed by a brief summary of how hate speech frequently is protected as free speech.

1.1 A Working Definition and Focus

Working definition: *Hate speech comprises any form of hateful or contemptuous expression that attacks, degrades, or vilifies people based on their social identities.*

Focus: *Hate speech targeting social identities that are devalued by a society's dominant groups, and that is likely to evoke, promote, or legitimize harms such as violence, discrimination, and oppression.*

This working definition and focus draw upon prior expositions, including:

- *words that are used as weapons to ambush, terrorize, wound, humiliate, and degrade* (Matsuda et al., 1993)

- *speech likely to produce the effect of legitimising, spreading or promoting racial hatred, xenophobia, anti-Semitism or other forms of discrimination or hatred based on intolerance* (Council of Europe Committee of Ministers, 1997)

- *the expression of hate and/or the encouragement of violence against others based on their real or assumed membership in a given category* (Cervone, Augoustinos, & Maass, 2021)

- *oral and written communication, as well as the use of symbols, parades, and other visual or nonverbal forms of expression* (Ruscher, 2001)

- *a form of derogatory language directed particularly at groups evoking contempt* (Bilewicz & Soral, 2020)

- *content that promotes violence or hatred against individuals or groups based on any of the following attributes, which indicate a protected group status under YouTube's policy (Age, Caste, Disability, Ethnicity, Gender Identity and Expression, Nationality, Race, Immigration Status, Religion, Sex/ Gender, Sexual Orientation, Victims of a Major Violent Event and Their Kin, Veteran Status)* (YouTube, 2019).

Four features in the current working definition and focus are worthy of note. First, hate speech is a *hateful or contemptuous attack* based on *social identities*: It is different from a nonspecific derogatory insult as well as from a mere category reference (Bianchi et al., 2019). The attack on social identity distinguishes hate speech from overlapping concepts such as toxic language and profanity (Chhabra & Vishwakarma, 2022), and the attack is *hateful* – divisive, bigoted, vile, and intolerant – rather than merely impolite or rude (Culpeper, 2021). Second, although "speech" implies spoken words, hate speech is understood to be *any form of hateful expression*: spoken words, tweets, song lyrics, symbols, memes, photos, or gestures, to name a few. Third, hate speech is a tool *typically employed by dominant social groups* against less powerful social groups. As most of the quoted definitions above assert or imply, hate speech targets lower status groups such as immigrants or religious, ethnic, and sexual minorities. These are the groups that typically evoke contempt and disgust from higher status groups (i.e., low in both warmth and competence; Fiske, 2018). Finally, hate speech is highly likely to produce *harm*. It negatively affects targets themselves with humiliation, fear, and silencing. Hate speech also produces effects on observers (e.g., stereotype activation) as well as society-level effects, such as legitimizing discrimination and promoting group-level hatred and violence (even if communicated in settings where targets do not directly encounter it).

More narrow approaches admittedly are conceivable. For example, one could restrict consideration of hate speech to what is illegal in the country of interest. For example, although reasonable laypersons might view cross-burning on the lawn of a Black/African American family as hate speech, it may not be technically illegal in all cases. In *R.A.V.* v. *City of St. Paul, 1992*, the city ordinance prohibiting such behavior was declared as unconstitutional because it only prohibited use of threatening symbols against certain types of groups, but not others (i.e., differential treatment of groups is not "content-neutral" according to the US Supreme Court). An alternative example in the Netherlands shows how hate speech sometimes is legal despite a hate speech ban: Although the Dutch far-right politician Geert Wilders was charged for anti-Muslim hate speech, he ultimately was acquitted partly on the grounds that politicians need to voice the ideas on which they might act, if elected (van Noorloos, 2013). Conversely, a broader approach might be employed. For example, one could omit the idea that hate speech is used primarily by powerful groups to produce humiliation, fear, and delegitimization. But from this author's perspective, there is something fundamentally different about hateful language used by oppressive high-status groups versus the lower-status groups that are exploited, oppressed, or killed. It is analogous to recognizing that aggression initiated to achieve harm is different than aggressive behavior enacted in self-defense. There may be points of overlap (e.g., both high- and low-status groups may use derogatory group terms for each other), but with a focus on hate speech as a tool to maintain power and status (e.g., Carlson, 2021), power asymmetry is a relevant boundary feature.

An even broader approach would include indirect or subtle expression across the full range of prejudiced and discriminatory communication. Medical professionals speak louder with exaggerated stress to nonnative language speakers (Woolfson, 1991), marketing companies may rely on advertising icons that appear to be male rather than female (Peirce & McBride, 1999), politicians may insist that nonracial justifications underlie positions that could negatively impact a racial minority (Thompson & Busby, 2023), people with cavalier beliefs about humor might find out-group-disparaging jokes funny (Hodson, Rush, & MacInnis, 2010), and individuals may display negative nonverbal behaviors toward someone from a sexual minority (Goodman et al., 2008). These examples may or may not be hate speech from the current perspective, depending on whether they attack social identity. But even if one or more of these examples are not hate speech per se, they could contribute to the prejudiced context in which hate speech thrives. Institutional leadership that overlooks patronizing speech to nonnative speakers or ignores gender bias in advertising campaigns, for example, may be tolerating a climate where more blatant harassment and hate speech can survive. Although discussion here centers on blatantly prejudiced communication, this Element occasionally will draw parallels from more subtle or ambiguous prejudiced communication (particularly as it contributes to the context in which hate speech occurs).

As evident from the expositions above, there is not a universally agreed-upon definition of hate speech (Hietanen & Eddebo, 2023). Is intent to harm a necessary feature or can harm derive from failure to be mindful? Do targets need to be aware that they and their group are harmed, or can harm occur downstream? Should a definition be constrained to the laws, ordinances, and policies operating in targets' and perpetrators' immediate environments, or should hate speech extend to lay understandings that may be more broad than formal injunctions? Taking a cue from computer-based hate speech detection (detailed in Section 5), one might designate something as hate speech when there is association between expressions of hate, contempt, or prescribed violence (e.g., from an established lexicon; through natural language processing) to a group (e.g., naming the group; #hashtagging a group-relevant topic). But, even then, is hate speech only relevant to specific protected groups (e.g., as in the YouTube policy noted above) or is hate speech relevant even when it targets hated harm-causing groups such as child molesters, rapists, or terrorists (Crandall, Eshelman, & O'Brien, 2002)? Who decides which, if any, groups might understandably be targeted with expressions of extreme hate? Does it depend on their current potential to cause harm to others (e.g., freely operating in society versus during incarceration)?

Answers to these questions may vary across societies and across time . . . and are well beyond the scope of this Element (hence the focus on hate speech used as a tool by socially dominant groups that has high potential to cause harm). The intention of a working definition and focus here is not to claim a decisive solution to long-standing challenges in defining hate speech, but rather to provide scope and boundary for the current work.

1.2 Hate Speech and Free Speech

Freedom of speech and expression are recognized as fundamental human rights in Article 19 of the Universal Declaration of Human Rights (United Nations General Assembly, 1948). Although not binding in the strictest legal sense, the Declaration and documents derived from it reflect a widespread value for freedom of expression. That said, there can be restrictions on speech as well as limits on what restrictions can be imposed, and these are relevant for consideration of hate speech. Internet websites such as YouTube, for example, may have "terms of use" policies that prohibit hate speech (see above). Conversely, the First Amendment of the US Constitution (Amendment 1.7) prohibits Congress from making laws that abridge freedom of speech, but also notes exceptions such as speech that reflects "a clear and present danger" or "fighting words" that will provoke immediate violence (Cornell Law School, US Constitution Annotated). Similarly, the UK's Racial and Religious Hatred Act of 2006 prohibits stirring up hatred against persons on racial or religious grounds, but does not restrict expressions of antipathy or criticism (i.e., stirring up hatred purportedly goes beyond expressing negative viewpoints). Thus, hate speech might be prohibited (and even illegal) in some circumstances but unrestricted in others.

Even when hate speech is not prohibited per se, it may co-occur with the violation of other laws, or provide evidence for a violation. Hate speech might be evident in cases of discrimination, including prohibitions against hostile environments that interfere with education or employment (see Titles VI and VII of the US Civil Rights Act of 1964). For example, in *Harris* v. *Forklift Systems 1993*, the US Supreme Court ruled that pervasive and repeated gender-based insults contributed to hostile work environment (for a discussion, see Leskinen, Rabelo, & Cortina, 2015). In prosecution of criminal law, hate speech might be used to demonstrate a perpetrator's bias, which is required for a hate crime designation. Hate crimes in the United States (for a discussion, see Roussos & Dovidio, 2018) and the UK (for a discussion, see Bacon, May, & Charlesford, 2021) are expected to carry a heavier penalty than the same crime without the hate crime designation. For example, in a report on successful hate crime prosecutions, the UK's Crown Prosecution Service (2023) reported that racial abuse by a defendant who was consuming alcohol in an alcohol-free zone raised what ordinarily is a noncustodial sentence to twelve weeks prison time. (Thus, even if hate speech per se may be "free speech," it can be used to document malicious intent, pervasiveness, and pattern.)

2 Forms of Hate Speech

Hate speech can take many forms. In verbal expression, it can be found in derogatory group labels, dehumanizing metaphors, and negative exemplars which, by extension, prescribe a course of action (e.g., vermin must be exterminated). Visual representations may draw upon metaphors or may rely upon threatening symbols. The expression of hate speech can be in-person, via openly available mass communication, or tucked away on fringe websites and social media platforms. It may be veridically attributed to a specific source or may be anonymous.

The varied forms and media discussed below – derogatory group labels, metaphors, exemplification, visual repretentations – are neither mutually exclusive nor exhaustive. Some metaphors, for example, rely on visual representation and may evoke stereotypic exemplars. Several features cut across the forms of hate speech, including sheer vitriol, patterns of "othering," and willful use of faulty reasoning. With respect to vitriol, hate speech includes extreme negative affect, blaming, demonizing, and calls to violence. An analysis of social media posts about Ethiopian political strife provides an extreme illustration (Chekol, Moges, & Nigatu, 2023): *"The devil itself learns conspiracy from Tigray; if there is Tigray, there is stealing."* The generalization about this ethnic minority group's purported negative behavior and a thinly veiled attribution of evil clearly conveys hatred and contempt. Similarly, an analysis of Twitter messages to feminist podcaster Anita Sarkeesian are replete with explicit rape threats and venomously misogynistic assertions about women (Hopton & Langer, 2021). Across its myriad forms, the negativity of hate speech may be as transparent as asserting that a group is an evil band of blithering idiots or as opaque as using coded language only understood fully by a hate group. But the negativity carries across its various forms of expression in group labels used, metaphors evoked, examples proffered, and images rendered.

As an attack on social identity, hate speech also involves "othering." Othering can involve representation of an out-group as different or as a threat, or by failing to represent the out-group at all (Chauhan & Foster, 2013). The out-group is not merely different, but is characterized as inferior with respect to moral and/or ability characteristics (discussed more in Section 3.2). With respect to perceived threat, hate speech often involves dehumanizing out-groups as animals or parasite/viruses (discussed more in Section 2.2). A notable example from Hitler's *Mein Kampf* reads "[*the Jew] is and remains the typical parasite, a sponger who, like an infectious bacillus, keeps spreading*" (Musolff, 2007). As discussed in Sections 2.1, 2.2, 2.3, and 2.4, the dehumanizing theme appears in group labels, metaphors, and use of exemplars or visual images. Finally, one can consider failure to represent a group as a kind of othering and, sometimes, as constituting hate speech. Objectification, for example, regards an out-group as a tool or discardable nuisance, rather than as an agentic human being (see Sections 2.1 and 3.2). Alternatively, ignoring or failing to see the potential impact of toxic narratives or labels – as if the group were invisible or irrelevant – can allow the perpetuation of hate speech. Thus, hate speech need not derive from a conscious intent to harm. Finally, denial that horrific acts of violence were perpetrated against a group (e.g., Holocaust denial) is an extreme example of othering via failure to represent. Such denial arguably constitutes hate speech (Cohen-Almagor, 2008).

Also cutting across forms of hate speech is the evidence of cognitive stereotype-supporting biases on the part of the communicator (for a discussion of these biases, see Fiske, 1998). For example, perpetrators of hate speech may show signs of the illusory correlation bias, whereby they overestimate the co-occurrence of rarities (i.e., extremely rare negative behaviors are associated with numerically small minorities, for example, the discussion of Romani and immigrants in Section 2.3). They also may be sensitive to stereotype-confirming information, interpreting events through the lens of what they already believe and bolstering those beliefs among others through hate speech. The labels, exemplars, and images communicated through hate speech exaggerate the differences between the communicator's in-group and the disparaged out-group and also minimize differences within the out-group (i.e., out-group homogeneity effect). Again, hate speech often involves stereotype communication but stereotype communication is neither necessary (e.g., rejoicing about deaths among an out-group fails to convey a stereotype) nor sufficient (e.g., expressing an opinion the librarians are introverted does not appear viciously hateful) to constitute hate speech.

Next is a (nonexhaustive) compendium of what hate speech can look like.

2.1 Derogatory Group Labels

Perhaps hate speech is best epitomized by derogatory group labels: labels that constitute the simplistic negative "othering" of the person and their group, implicating inferior social class, ethnicity, and nationality (e.g., Loughnan et al., 2014; Rice et al., 2010). Their use is commonly seen in ethnic slurs and group-level name calling. Some group epithets further convey the "functions" that allegedly inferior groups serve relative to the dominant group, essentially characterizing the disparaged group as mere objects to be used rather than as human beings. It is important to bear in mind that not all group labels or epithets comprise hate speech. There is nothing inherently derisive about referencing people as *upper division students*, *Mets fans*, or *Belgians*. Indeed, some epithets are generated or adopted by the group (e.g., Buffalo Bills fans self-reference as the *Bills Mafia*). If it is not a vicious attack on a social identity, it is unlikely to be perceived or experienced as hate speech.

Group epithets often cluster around physical characteristics, easily observed customs, and proper names; the number and complexity of epithets vary as a function of relative group size (Mullen & Johnson, 1993); when those epithets are perceived negatively, they function as derogatory group labels. All types of epithets can be perceived negatively. For example, negative epithets for Italian people include *meatball*, *wop*, and *Tony* (Rice et al., 2010). An epithet's use may develop over time, acquire origin stories, and might become archaic or extinguish entirely. *Wop*, for example, originally may have been a mean-spirited mimicry of young male Italian immigrants greeting each other with "*Guapo!*," but it also has been alleged to reflect illegal entry to the United States during the early twentieth century (i.e., **without papers**; Zimmer, 2018). The latter origin story conceivably gained traction precisely because the term derogates along moral and ability dimensions: European Americans who had already settled in the United States may have regarded Italian immigrants – particularly those from southern Italy – as unskilled, poor, and inferior (Cerase, 1974). Anecdotal observation suggests that ethnic slurs about Italian Americans may have declined over the past century, perhaps because Italian immigrants eventually identified as White upon arrival and that identity facilitated upward mobility (Guglielmo, 2004). Although epithets and the groups targeted by them change over time, propagating a group's inferiority with derogatory group labels is a tried-and-true conveyor of hate speech.

Socially inferior people also are easily objectified into things to be used. Objectification denies a person's humanity, and instead involves treating the person as a means to an end (Orehek & Weavering, 2017), and the terms that signify "functional" objectification are attacks on social identity that punctuate the superiority (and unequivocal humanity) of the dominant group. As such, a member of the dominant group feels authorized to use objectified others to achieve goals, and to ignore objectified others' autonomy, agency, and right to personal boundaries. Sexual objectification of women is a common example. Sexualized terms for women far outnumber sexualized terms for men (Stanley, 1973, cited in Spender, 1980), and many such terms explicitly describe how women are to be used (e.g., *piece of ass*). More recent empirical studies extend sexual objectification to sexual minorities (e.g., Szymanski, Mikorski, & Dunn, 2019) and gender minorities (Anzani et al., 2021). Members of racial and ethnic minority groups also are labeled as objects. Notably, calling an adult Black man *boy* directly references an era in which Black people were enslaved by White people (i.e., the individual is someone's "boy" who caters to their various demands; Ruscher, 2001); customarily used during slavery and segregation to reinforce subordinate status, courts and friends of the courts have recognized the use of *boy* as discriminatory and offensive (Amici Curiae Brief for 08–16135-BB). Referring to White people of low socioeconomic status as *White trash* literally asserts that they have no useful function in society (Loughnan et al., 2014). Other examples of derogatory labels that situate group members in terms of their functions (or lack thereof) include *coolie* for people of Asian descent (a term from the European colonial period for day laborers of Asian or East Indian descent) and *welfare queen* for unemployed African American mothers (who ostensibly garner social services to obtain a cushy lifestyle in lieu of working). Such terms connote the low ability, low status, and immoral qualities that the dominant group ascribes to the disparaged groups. As discussed in Section 4, derogatory group labels have myriad negative impacts, including emotional harm to targets as well as activation of stereotypes among observers.

2.2 Metaphors

Some derogatory group labels such as "ape" or "white trash" draw upon metaphors. Metaphors draw a symbolic parallel between a target and a source concept (Lakoff & Johnson, 1980; Landau, Meier, & Keefer, 2010). The target concept is what the communicator is attempting to illustrate, capture, or explain; in the case of hate speech, the disparaged group is the target concept. In contrast, the source concept is typically easily understood, familiar, and often evocatively rich. Examples include depicting African American people as nonhuman primates, describing ethnic minority groups as vermin or disease, or characterizing an uptick in immigration as a flood.

This last characterization – immigration as a flood – punctuates the fact that not all metaphors are derogatory group labels. And some derogatory group labels (e.g., wop) are not obvious metaphors.

Some metaphors focus on a group-level threat in which the disparaged group operates as a single entity or event: The dominant in-group's home country or city essentially is a body or container that is overcome by the disparaged group. For example, the health of the nation-as-body is threatened by the disparaged group characterized as a plague of vermin or spreading cancer. Alternatively, the perceived impact of disparaged group may be characterized as a flood that overwhelms the dominant system. The system buckles with the pressures of increased demands and remains ruined even after the waters have receded (e.g., Charteris-Black, 2006; El Refaie, 2001). Flooding rains, failing dams, and the aftermath of mud and mold strike chords of dread with many audiences, all the while avoiding racially charged language. Jimenez, Arendt, and Landau (2021) present an especially provocative example of how powerful the inundation metaphor can be. First, they showed that actual Twitter posts supporting a border wall between the United States and Mexico used the inundation metaphor more than anti-immigration posts that did not mention a wall (or posts that opposed a wall); an example that they provide of #BuildTheWall reads: "*If we were to go by @RepHankJohnson logic, the #USA should sink with all the illegal immigrants piling into it which would cause it to flood.*" Second, they experimentally examined the impact of the inundation metaphor on support for a border wall. When potential economic threats of undocumented immigration were cast in terms of inundation metaphor, rather than a purely literal description, US participants reported greater support for a border wall (statistically controlling for conservatism and Trump support). A group-level threat prompted advocacy of a group-level solution. In this case, create a barrier.

Another group-level metaphor casts the disparaged group as a public health threat: a swarm of destructive insects, an infestation of vermin, or a crippling disease. Adolf Hitler regularly used the public health metaphor in speeches about Jewish people, conceptualizing them as parasites and disease from which the national body of Germany needed to be cured (Musolff, 2007). Empirical work by Esses and her colleagues (Esses, Medianu, & Lawson, 2013) demonstrates that such metaphors remain powerful in contemporary society. They presented participants with a neutral article in which a political cartoon appeared (purportedly incidental) on the same page. In this cartoon, disembarking immigrants carried suitcases either with diseases labeled on them (e.g., SARS, AIDS) or had no printing on the suitcases. Although participants rarely reported remembering the cartoon, those exposed to the disease suitcases reported greater contempt toward immigrants, expressed dehumanizing beliefs about them, saw immigrants as spreaders of disease, and reported more negative attitudes about immigrants and immigration. A long tradition in social sciences shows that attitudes can influence overt behaviors (Glasman & Albarracín, 2006 for a review), so negative attitudes such as these may contribute to relevant overt anti-immigrant behaviors such as voting against liberal policies, re-tweeting anti-immigrant stories, and evincing hiring bias (to name a few). Metaphors such as these also seem to affect the mental representation of the disparaged group, facilitating the comprehension of metaphor-congruent information. Tipler (2016) showed that participants who repeatedly were exposed to statements that evoke the immigrants-as-parasites metaphor (e.g., *Our nation is full of immigrant vermin*) later evinced slower reading time of metaphor-incongruent statements (e.g., *Immigrants are self-sufficient*). That is, people could not easily think of immigrants as anything but vermin. This relation, in turn, increased anti-immigrant resource attitudes (e.g., *Immigrants need to be prevented from taking jobs away from regular Americans*). Once people latch onto a hate speech metaphor, they do not easily switch to other ways of thinking about the disparaged group.

Vermin and parasite metaphors are distinctly dehumanizing metaphors. Dehumanization involves the failure to ascribe human characteristics to certain individuals and groups. In one prominent framework, fully human beings have qualities of both human nature (e.g., curiosity, emotionality) and human uniqueness (e.g., rationality; Haslam et al., 2005). From this framework, vermin and parasites are attributed qualities of neither human nature nor human uniqueness. In another prominent framework that draws from the Stereotype Content Model (Fiske, 2018), dehumanization is a function of how likeable and how competent a group is (Harris & Fiske, 2006). From this framework, groups construed as vermin or parasites would be disliked immensely, seen as acting without intelligence (i.e., low competence), and regarded with genuine disgust. A more recent framework (Tipler & Ruscher, 2014) explicitly connects dehumanization to metaphors, and considers a group's perceived capacity for affective, cognitive, and behavioral agency. In this dehumanizing metaphor framework, out-groups viewed as vermin and parasites simply evince behavior (i.e., they swarm or leech off the system) and do not elicit attributions of affective or cognitive states; as with the Harris and Fiske framework, such out-groups elicit disgust.

Another prominent dehumanizing metaphor used in hate speech involves the insidious comparison of people of African descent to nonhuman primates (Lott, 1999). The ancient Greeks and Romans characterized nonhuman primates as incomplete humans, and medieval Christians placed humans between angels and apes on the Chain of Being (Panaitiu, 2020). Nonhuman primates purportedly lack higher cognitive abilities, with their behaviors driven by the need to satisfy immediate desires (Tipler & Ruscher, 2014). Early anthropological writings by Europeans included arguments that explicitly dehumanized Black people in this way, such as not being descended from biblical Adam, and as having posture somewhere between bipeds and quadrupeds (Panaitiu, 2019). By the time of the 3/5th compromise in 1787 (i.e., that 3/5 of the enslaved population would be counted to determine a state's representation in Congress), the idea that African descended peoples were not fully human was well established in the United States.

Contemporarily, both Barack Obama (Joseph, 2011) and Michelle Obama (Kendall, 2016) have been portrayed publicly as nonhuman primates. But the Black–ape association is not "merely" anecdotal: An archival study of 1979–1999 *Philadelphia Inquirer* articles about death-qualified cases found ape-relevant language more commonly used for Black than for White defendants (Goff et al., 2008). The ape–Black association also may contribute to perceptions that aggressively subduing Black suspects is justified. In another of the Goff et al. studies (2008), White participants subliminally primed with ape-relevant words (as opposed to words relevant to big cats such as tigers) perceived more justification for police violence toward a Black suspect. A similar pattern is observed in judgments of culpability among Black children: Ape-relevant primes increase culpability for Black children accused of felonies relative to misdemeanors (Goff et al., 2014). Thus, once characterized or associated with nonhuman primates – unevolved, ignorant, violent, buffoonish, and ungraceful – the communicator justifies denial of full participation in a free society. Metaphors thus comprise a powerful and effective strategy for hate speech.

2.3 Exemplification

Exemplification theory proposes that communication – particularly in the context of the news media – uses a handful of exemplars or instances to illustrate and persuade about a larger phenomenon (Zillman, 1999). Relative to messaging with mere base rate information or without exemplars, exemplar-based messaging exerts stronger effects on attitudes, intentions, and behavior (Bigsby, Bigman, & Gonzalez, 2019). Not surprisingly, then, hate speech sometimes leverages the power of exemplars to illustrate the communicator's point about a disparaged group. The exemplars need not be representative – nor even factual – as long as the prototypical features fit the point at hand.

Characterization of the Romani (often referenced with the derogatory term *gypsy*) provides a good illustration of exemplification. A few well-circulated stories about Romani may fail to capture the range of activities by large numbers of Romani in a particular district ... but those stories assuredly will illustrate purported negative attributes (Tileagă, 2007). Stories allege that Romani must be dragged to school, that they ruin facilities bestowed upon them magnanimously by the government, and that they consume and destroy resources like rats (Tileagă, 2007). As seen with illusory correlation, relatively rare (often negative) behaviors are seen as prevalent among a statistical minority group. Exemplification also is seen in US stories that circulated about particular Latinx immigrants. For instance, the *Virginia Gazette* in 2006 repeatedly referenced two high-profile cases of male Latinx immigrants charged in local deaths. One case involved the rape and murder of a young girl, and the other case involved a DUI in which two young girls were killed (Sohoni & Sohoni, 2014). The not-at-all-subtle repeated message is that Latinx immigrants are dangerous criminals. Similarly, speeches by presidential candidate Donald Trump regularly invoked negative Latinx exemplars. One such exemplar involved illegal Latinx immigrants accused of beating a ninety-year-old man to death (Lamont, Park, & Ayala-Hurtado, 2017). Through exemplification, a communicator conflates perceived relations among criminality, illegal entry, and immigration. In reality, not all immigrants at the southern US border enter illegally. In addition, violation of civil law does not connote criminality, and most immigrants are not violent criminals. But from a few instances with shared features, people who hear the exemplified stories will aggregate information into a prototypical pattern (Nisbett et al., 1983). Ultimately, listeners will judge the whole of the group by some of its (alleged) parts (Zillman, 1999) and confirm their expectations about the group.

High profile examples can include exaggeration and fabrication. The case of the *Tampa* is a good illustration. In 2001, as it approached Australia, the Norwegian vessel *Tampa* had rescued a group of Indonesian asylum seekers on the open seas. After the government's initial denial of asylum, some newspapers claimed that asylum seekers threw their children overboard because, in international waters, the navy would be obliged to rescue them from drowning. Once rescued, the narrative alleged, refuge in Australia would necessarily be provided. As evidence, news outlets provided photos that showed Indonesian people in the open waters. Fueling the controversy, the then electoral candidate John Howard signaled that such callous individuals were unworthy of welcome to Australia. But the story later was shown to be false (Curran, 2004); the photos of people in the water apparently recorded the initial rescue *not* callous manipulation attempts by the Indonesian asylum seekers. By then, of course, the damage was done: Negative public opinion against the asylum seekers held for quite some time. Once moral failures are believed, it is difficult to disconfirm or "walk them back" (Rothbart & Park, 1986).

2.4 Visual Representations

The case of the *Tampa* is a chilling example of how images can be used in the service of hate speech. Relative to video images from legitimate sources, video images from faked news sources may exert stronger impacts on relevant intergroup attitudes and beliefs (C. Wright et al., 2021). Photographs or video footage can be misattributed, edited with technology, and completely fabricated. In fact, people may share images that they know to be false, especially if they desperately wish to remain engaged in the conversations of their social circles (Ahmed, 2022). Visual representations can punctuate an exemplar, as in the *Tampa* case, as well as operating as visual metaphors. Alternatively, visual representations can comprise part of a group-disparaging meme, usually an image with sarcastic or ironic captioning (e.g., Døving & Emberland, 2021; Duchscherer & Dovidio, 2016; Merritt, O'Brien, & Ruscher, 2021); internet memes can spread rapidly, and can be "mutated" as into new incarnations as they spread (Wiggins & Browers, 2014). Cartoons, which similarly comprise a mixture of words and images, also are vehicles of hate speech. In a highly publicized event, the Danish newspaper *Jyllands-Posten* published cartoons of the Prophet Muhammed, including one depicting a bomb in his turban (Al-Rawi, 2015); beyond the abusive content per se, the representation can be doubly offensive, insofar as some branches of Islam prohibit such visual depictions of the Prophet. Circling back to a previously-discussed example of out-group disparagement, the ape metaphor often is presented via offensive caricatures and visual allusions. Joseph (2011) recounts how a caller to a Rush Limbaugh radio program alleged a similarity between President Obama and the children's book character Curious George; after that call, a local bar owner began to sell Obama/Curious George shirts. Besides being the depiction of a nonhuman creature with primitive qualities and nominal intellect, Joseph (2011) notes that Curious George – stolen from Africa by a White man – serves as an analogy for slavery. Pivoting to another variant of the ape metaphor – an uncivilized lustful beast – a controversial 2008 *Vogue* cover depicted basketball great LeBron James and supermodel Gisele Bundchen – a Black man and a blonde White woman – in a pose that is unmistakably evocative of the film *King Kong* (Desai, 2010). Several variants of the ape metaphor thus appear to be alive and well in contemporary society, and are well positioned to convey offensive messages.

Even without offensive metaphors or inflammatory stories, visual representations as hate speech can perpetuate toxic narratives. A notable example comprises the use of Native American mascots for athletic teams. Such mascots both assert that Native American people are irrelevant in contemporary society, and that they are inferior subhumans (Dai et al., 2021). In providing guidelines about use of Native American mascots in 2005, the National Collegiate Athletic Association (NCAA) explicitly banned mascots, nicknames, and images that were "hostile in terms of race, ethnicity, or national origin" at championship events (Williams, 2005). Although this prohibition extends to uniforms and paraphernalia displayed by players, cheerleaders, and band members, it does not extend to nonchampionship events nor to spectators at any events. That said, the NCAA ban was a small first step toward recognizing that the use of Native American mascots has critical features of hate speech. An illustration of the controversy about mascot and name changes is evident in professional sports, namely, in the controversy about the National Football League (NFL) team currently affiliated with Washington, DC (called the *Redskins* until July 2020). Using data from the 2014 Cooperative Congressional Election Study, Sharrow and colleagues reported that fewer than 25 percent of respondents considered the name offensive or supported a name change (Sharrow, Tarsi, & Nteta, 2021). However, Sharrow et al. also reported that the perception that *Redskins* was inoffensive increased as a function of symbolic racism against Native Americans. Similarly, opposition to a name change also increased as a function of symbolic racism. Thus, those highest in prejudice preferred to continue the toxic narrative.

Finally, symbols and symbolic gestures can be forms of hate speech. Continuing with the example of Native American mascots, the symbolic gesture of the "tomahawk chop" performed by spectators at sporting events (e.g., Atlanta Braves; Kansas City Chiefs) casts native people as brutal and subhuman savages (Dai et al., 2021). Although symbols can mean different things to different people across different contexts and eras, the reasonable person may recognize when a particular symbol might be threatening. For example, in *R. A. V.* v. *the City of St. Paul*, a cross was constructed and set ablaze in front of the home of an African American family, and therefore viewed by the lower courts as violating the ordinance. As noted earlier, the higher courts invalidated the ordinance because it specified some groups but not others. But being legally protected as free speech does not negate a burning cross as symbolic hate speech. Hate speech also may be expressed by symbols and gestures that signify violence and excessive prejudice, such as nooses, swastikas, or gestures that communicate exaggerated inferiority and disposability based on group membership. The symbols may or may not be legal, but they are expressions that attack particular identity groups.

2.5 Summary

In the working definition, hate speech *"comprises any form of hateful or contemptuous expression that attacks, degrades, or vilifies people based on their social identities."* Myriad forms of expression assault social identities: derogatory epithets, pictures and stories, metaphor and symbol. Out-groups are inferior, contemptuous, dangerous, and morally excluded. These portraits of hate speech – what hate speech looks like – only lightly touched upon why it occurs: the dominant group's claims to superiority and relevance, protection of territory and position, and long-standing prejudice. The next section provides a more in-depth look at why hate speech occurs.

3 Factors Contributing to Hate Speech

Hate speech can be construed as a specific type of discrimination. As such, it reflects differential treatment based on group characteristics: referring to someone by a derogatory category label, perpetuating or tolerating dehumanizing metaphors, or policies that fail to protect against or prohibit hate speech. As a type of discrimination, hate speech is predicted by many underlying causes for other forms of discrimination: It can derive from personal prejudices or negative emotions, real or symbolic group conflict, and structural features of society. Thus, some underlying causes for hate speech operate primarily at the level of individual speakers, whereas some precipitating factors lie squarely within group-level phenomena. And some explanations and sequelae – although traceable to the behaviors of individuals and groups – are best examined at a structural or institutional level. It is important to note that these levels are not mutually exclusive. For example, intergroup conflict could evoke hate speech most easily from individuals who are high in prejudice, particularly in contexts that tolerate its expression.

3.1 Individual-Level Factors

Individual-level explanations for prejudice and discrimination have a long-standing history in social psychology. Whether deriving from transient mood states or enduring characteristics of the person, individual-level factors prompt particular people to be more or less likely to behave in a discriminatory fashion. By extension, some people are more or less likely to express or tolerate hate speech. Fiske (1998) notes that most individual-level explanations for prejudice primarily focus on personality characteristics or individual differences, and she traces the historical focus on individual prejudices to work on the authoritarian personality in the late 1940s in the wake of the Holocaust. Individual differences in overtly negative attitudes – the so-called old-fashioned prejudice – against various social groups predict blatantly obvious discrimination in an array of domains. These domains included employment, housing, and service in retail and dining establishments. By the 1970s, however, researchers shifted their focus. Rather than studying overtly prejudiced attitudes, researchers focused on the "modern prejudices" that reflected tension between longstanding negative attitudes and standards to behave in a nondiscriminatory fashion (e.g., Devine et al., 1991). For example, White people high in modern racism especially experience this tension. They simultaneously want to maintain their egalitarian self-views but are plagued by a discomfort interacting with Black people in contemporary society. Consequently, White people high in modern racism may not show overt retaliatory aggression toward a Black person (e.g., via noise burst intensity) but will increase retaliatory aggression that is nonobvious or covert (e.g., via noise burst duration; Beal et al., 2000). With respect to discriminatory language, research during the "modern prejudice" period focused on how individual differences predicted subtle patterns such as linguistic intergroup bias (e.g., characterizing negative behaviors with abstract adjectives such as *uncivilized* or *dirty* rather than with concrete expressions such as *spoke loudly* or *had dirt on his hands*; Schnake & Ruscher, 1998) or the use of discriminatory labels when cognitive capacity necessary to censor one's own biased communication is diminished (e.g., referring to women as *babes* or *girls* when cognitively busy; Cralley & Ruscher, 2005). Individuals high in modern prejudice essentially leak discriminatory behavior when the behavior being measured is subtle, difficult to control, or covert. Hate speech, in contrast, arguably is neither subtle nor uncontrollable. And even if the source may be occluded, the hateful message typically is not missed by the intended audience.

In the past decade or so, social science researchers have returned to an examination of obvious and overt discrimination (e.g., racial bias in decisions to shoot; for a review, see Payne & Correll, 2020). As evident from the Web of Science data noted in the opening paragraphs, scholars' interest in hate speech is not far behind. One reasonably would expect that individual differences in old-fashioned prejudice would predict hate speech and extreme discriminatory language ... but empirical published work currently is scant. It may be that the hypothesis is too obvious to prompt research and publication, insofar as it borders on tautological (e.g., people with openly expressed antipathy toward members of group X will refer to them by derogatory group labels). Or, to the extent that individual expressions of hate speech do not fall along a normal distribution, researchers may face unfamiliar statistical analysis that steers them away from this topic. Alternatively, potential participants might decline to respond to transparent surveys about their own prejudice and discriminatory language. But recognizing that some people are unabashedly open about their prejudices, Forscher and colleagues (Forscher et al., 2015) proposed an individual difference called *Motivation to Express Prejudice* (MP) that includes items such whether one should or does express negative thoughts and feelings about a particular group. As anticipated, MP predicts blatant discrimination (e.g., support for political candidates who endorse oppressive policies) and prejudiced affect (e.g., feeling thermometers) and is posited by Forscher and colleagues to predict other intentional behaviors such as hate speech. Another measure, *Acceptability of Racial Microaggressions Scale* (ARMS), comprises perceptions that it is acceptable for White people to blame other racial groups for negative outcomes, express colorblindness, or deny systemic racism even when speaking with racially diverse audiences (Mekawi & Todd, 2018). Acceptability of Racial Microaggressions Scale subscales correlate with prejudiced attitudes (e.g., modern racism). Similarly, the *Sex-Based Harassment Inventory* (Grabowski et al., 2022) includes items such as likelihood of telling sexist jokes and using sexist slurs; it correlates with hostile sexism. In short, there are individual differences in beliefs that people should, will, and wish to express their various prejudices aloud.

Another individual difference linked to discrimination is *Social Dominance Orientation* (SDO), which reflects a stable preference for maintaining group hierarchies and social inequality (Pratto et al., 1994). Not surprisingly, SDO typically is higher in groups that hold greater social power – men and members of dominant racial/ethnic groups in various nations (Lee, Pratto, & Johnson, 2011) – the very groups posited to benefit directly or indirectly from hate speech. As well as other discriminatory behaviors (e.g., hiring recommendations, Hansen & Dovidio, 2016), SDO correlates with the aforementioned ARMS, which supports the expression of prejudiced beliefs. Social Dominance Orientation also predicts dehumanization of immigrants both directly and indirectly through a perception that humans are different from other animals (Costello & Hodson, 2009). Perceiving immigrants as resembling nonhuman animals is a logical precursor to depicting them as such through metaphoric hate speech and derogatory animalistic labels.

Although published empirical work has yet to report that those higher in SDO are more likely to *express* hate speech themselves, several studies suggest that SDO predicts *tolerance* of hate speech perpetrated by others. People higher in SDO are more tolerant of blatantly discriminatory behaviors perpetrated by other people (e.g., Gutierrez & Unzueta, 2021) and are less supportive of hate speech prohibitions (Bilewicz et al., 2017). In one illustrative study, business student participants observed an online chat session between their coworkers

(Rosette et al., 2013). Within the chat, coworkers made racial slurs about potential candidates who might join their working group. After each chat exchange, participants had the opportunity to provide feedback to their coworkers as well as to their senior executive. As SDO increased, the odds of remaining silent about others' racial slurs increased. This pattern of not speaking up is consistent with the notion that SDO predicts tolerance of hate speech. Moreover, failure to recognize or confront racist comments can be construed as a "secondary microaggression," insofar as such failure perpetuates the system in which such comments can persist (Johnson et al., 2021). Silence in the face of hate speech is complicity.

Tolerance for hate speech against women and sexual minorities also may be predicted by individual differences. Hostile sexism, for example, predicts tolerance of sexual harassment and gender-based harassment, which can include hate speech such as circulating sexist humor or using derogatory gendered labels (for review see Bareket & Fiske, 2023). Similarly, men's sexual harassment to strangers (e.g., cat-calls, sexualized comments) is predicted by high likelihood to sexually harass, particularly when men are with male peers rather than alone (Wesselmann & Kelly, 2010). Specifically addressing hate speech tolerance, Cowan and colleagues (Cowan et al., 2005) found that heterosexual college students' negative attitudes about homosexuality and their level of modern heterosexism predict attenuated judgments that hate speech directed toward gay men and lesbian women is harmful, and also predicted attenuated perceptions that specific violent anti-gay communications were offensive (e.g., a fraternity song about mutilating gays; a fraternity party in which members caricatured gay stereotypes). Again, tolerance is complicity, and helps maintain privileged positions of men in society as well as maintaining heteronormativity.

Individual difference constructs such as *Modern Prejudice, Motivation to Express Prejudice, Hostile Sexism*, and SDO assess relatively stable attitudinal patterns and behavioral inclinations that individuals carry with them across situations and time. There also are potential individual-level explanations for aggressive hate speech that derive from individual actors, but that *vary* across situations and time (e.g., states). Negative emotions such as anger or contempt are likely candidates. When anger and related constructs are examined as stable traits, they predict aggressive behavior, especially under provocation or threat (e.g., Bettencourt et al., 2006). More transient experiences of emotional animosity follow suit: Priming individuals with the combination of anger, contempt, and disgust is associated with aggressive behavior. Individuals primed with this combination generate more aggressive sentence completions (e.g., H_T is completed as HIT rather than HAT) and generate more anger and swear words than individuals in control conditions (Matsumoto, Hwang, & Frank, 2016); negative emotion-primed individuals also display more aggressive behavior toward out-groups (Matsumoto, Hwang, & Frank, 2017). In more naturalistic settings, politicians' speeches that express anger, contempt, and disgust toward out-groups predict the occurrence of intergroup-relevant violent events three to six months later (Matsumoto, Frank, & Hwang, 2015). The link among emotional animosity, hate speech, and violence would seem to epitomize a layperson's understanding of hate speech.

3.2 Group-Level Factors

Two inter-rated truths about human behavior constitute the foundation for understanding prejudice as a group-level phenomenon and, by extension, help social scientists think about prejudiced behavior such as hate speech. First, human beings categorize most things that they encounter in the world: animals into species, literature into genres, events into scripts or occasions, and fellow humans into groups (Fiske, 1998). Second, human beings live in groups, and in-group members coordinate with each other for mutual success and safety (Nature Human Behaviour editorial, 2018). Thus, humans categorize other humans into groups, with some humans belonging to the in-group and others belonging to an out-group. In-group members often are favored simply by virtue of their in-group membership. Out-group members sometimes, but not always, are disparaged, and disparagement is especially likely in the face of threat. Both in-group favoritism and out-group threat – real or symbolic – are the source of group-level explanations for discriminatory language and, in some cases, for hate speech.

According to social identity theory and its intellectual descendants (Tajfel & Turner, 1986; Turner & Oaks, 1989), the groups to which a person belongs are an important part of identity. Belonging to those groups holds emotional significance, providing opportunities for collective self-esteem (e.g., Houston & Andreopoulou, 2003) and in-group pride (e.g., Thomas et al., 2017). An important assumption of these theories is that intergroup comparison and the presence of an out-group are necessary to produce in-group favoritism. In-group favoritism reflects the superiority of the in-group, but that *relative* superiority may not be sufficient to produce the disparagement associated with hate speech: An inferior out-group member need not be dehumanized, nor cast as a convenient scapegoat for social problems, nor threatened with menacing symbols. The relative inferiority might manifest other discriminatory language patterns such as linguistic intergroup bias (Maass et al., 1989), noninclusive language (Bailey, Dovidio, &

LaFrance, 2022), or language that fails to acknowledge a group's existence or relevance (e.g., Fryberg & Eason, 2017); such discriminatory patterns can be problematic in their own right, but they may or may not be commissions of hate speech per se. That said, in-group favoritism appears to be more a matter of in-group love than of out-group hate (for meta-analytic support, see Balliet, Wu, & DeDreu, 2014), so the mere existence of an out-group may be necessary for hate speech, but it does not appear to be sufficient.

The addition of intergroup threat likely increases the odds of hate speech. Threats can be symbolic or realistic (Stephan & Stephan, 2000; Stephan, Ybarra, & Rosa, 2015). Realistic conflict may involve competition for tangible resources – jobs, housing, benefits, and land – as well as conflict over the power that jealously protects those resources (e.g., political position, educational opportunity). As Riek and colleagues note (Riek, Mania, & Gaertner, 2006), realistic threat to one's in-group can prompt discrimination by an individual in-group member even if that individual is not personally affected. Riek et al. cite national survey data showing that poor economic conditions coupled with large proportions of immigrants or minorities is associated with high levels of negative bias against those groups (Quillian, 1995). Language and discrimin-ation link both indirectly and directly to realistic threat. As discussed earlier (Section 2.2), the Esses, Medianu, and Lawson (2013) study showed that characterizing immigrants as a disease threat prompted contempt and dehuman-ization. In a more recent example, Huang and colleagues (Huang et al., 2022) noted that anti-Chinese rhetoric characterized Chinese and Asian people as a health threat during early stages of the COVID-19 pandemic (*ChinaVirus; KungFlu*). During this period, Huang et al. report a greater decrease in traffic to Asian restaurants that were located in Trump-supporting areas, compared to other restaurants (Huang et al., 2022). More directly, Italian university students primed with threat from immigrants (versus no threat) show greater linguistic intergroup bias toward Roma individuals, characterizing them with abstract negative terms rather than more concrete expressions (Albarello & Rubino, 2018). The pattern was evident when realistic threat was primed by blaming job scarcity on immigration or when symbolic threat (discussed in the next paragraph) was primed by highlighting differences in moral traditions and ideology. Although linguistic intergroup bias is not always hate speech, the Albarello and Rubino study demonstrates the causal impact that threat can have on language and communication.

As seen in the Albarello and Rubino (2018) study, discriminatory language also can be affected by symbolic threats. Whereas realistic threats involve tangible risks – physical harm or loss of resources such as jobs and territory– symbolic threats jeopardize less tangible aspects of group identity such as in-group values, worldview, or traditions. For example, interracial or same-sex marriage present few tangible costs to advocates of same-race or cross-sex marriage, but these marriages threaten (often religious) ideology about how marriage "should" be. Symbolic threats can increase aggressive proxy behaviors such as sticking pins into a virtual voodoo doll or assigning extremely difficult puzzle tasks to out-group members (Martínez, van Prooijen, & Van Lange, 2022), and those aggressive behaviors are mediated by the degree of intergroup hate. To the extent that hateful speech is an aggressive behavior, it is quite plausible that symbolic threats prompt hateful speech. The relation between hate speech and group-level threat also may be reciprocal: Threat conceivably produces hate speech but hate speech also may communicate the experience of threat. For example, slogans and images can exploit symbolic threats of immigrants changing a host country's "way of life." Consistent with this possibility, Schmuck and Matthes (2017) note that right-wing populist parties in Switzerland use the slogan *Maria Instead of Sharia* or images like minarets piercing the Swiss national flag. Rather than insinuating that immigrants affect crime, unemployment, or drain resources (i.e., potentially realistic threats), such symbolic threats simply suggest that immigrants' names and religion are unwelcome in the existing national culture.

Intergroup threats alternatively can be viewed in terms of qualitative differences in the type of harm that different threats pose, and these different threats may lend themselves to qualitatively unique derogatory labels, metaphors, and images. For example, Terror Management Theory has focused on how threats to worldview can affect a wide range of outcomes, including punishing transgressors and exacerbating in-group bias (for a review, see Kesebir & Pyszczynski, 2011). In the post-September 11 landscape, Pyszczynski and colleagues (Pyszczynski et al., 2006) noted contemporaneous rhetoric in parts of the Middle East referencing the United States as "The Great Satan" and the "Enemy of Allah." At the same time, the then President George W. Bush alluded to an "axis of evil" among certain foreign nations and called supporters of Islamic martyrdom "evil-doers." This type of rhetoric demonizes out-group members and justifies extreme violence toward them. Against this backdrop, when mortality threats were heightened, Iranian college students increased support for martyrdom in conflict with the United States; at the same time, conservative American college students increased support for using extreme military force in foreign conflicts under mortality salience threats. Rather than mere co-occurrence, one further might expect a reciprocal effect in which mortality threats increase demonizing language and demonizing language exacerbates mortality threats. Another qualitatively distinct type of threat involves contamination resulting from disease spread, compromised "racial purity," or violations of the "laws of nature." Drawing upon an evolutionary perspective, Cottrell and Neuberg (2005) associate contamination threats with disgust, avoidance or barriers, and purification efforts. Laws may attempt to maintain barriers (e.g., miscegenation laws; laws restricting same-sex marriage), with rhetoric supporting extreme purification efforts such as "ethnic cleansing." Empirical research linking contamination threats to labels, metaphors, and images of diseases, blood-poisoning, and parasites would be welcome.

As a final example, some potential conflicts derive from institutionally sanctioned asymmetric relationships within a social environment: men and women, supervisors and employees, "masters" and servants. Arguably, groups in the powerful position of these asymmetries recognize some need for members of groups in the lower power position (indeed, sometimes objectifying them as tools or assets). Bareket and Fiske (2023) discuss this type of asymmetry with respect to hostile and benevolent sexism. Hostile sexism views women as seeking power over men and as a threat to men's power; this type of conflict presumably lends itself to sexually violent or anger-charged labels such as man-eater or feminazi. In contrast, benevolent sexism views women as deserving cherished protection, as long as they conform to traditional gender roles; gender role-conforming women who do not present conflict likely are subject to terms of endearment or infantilization such as "baby". One might hazard the hypothesis that use of labels and metaphors in these types of asymmetric relationships have covaried historically with progression (and regression) of women's rights, collective action, and civil rights. On the whole, it is likely that the type of perceived threat prompts qualitatively distinct variations in hate speech or, alternatively, the qualitative variation may betray how an in-group perceives or wishes to frame a particular threat.

The threats purportedly presented by an out-group also can prompt hate speech to enhance cohesion among in-group members, manage the group's impression to external constituencies, and to recruit new like-minded members. Internet hate group sites epitomize these uses for hate speech. Hate group websites not surprisingly include extremist symbols (e.g., swastikas), links to supremacist literature (e.g., *Mein Kampf*), and economic grievances (for examples see Gerstenfeld, Grant, & Chiang, 2003). More interestingly, sites also may endeavor to deny or reframe out-group threats: They may explicitly disavow racial hatred (Gerstenfeld, Grant, & Chiang, 2003), cast themselves as victims whose civil rights are jeopardized because they "merely" show White pride (Berbrier, 2000), and portray their group as the true champions of equality by virtue of a professed colorblind ideology (Gerstenfeld, Grant, & Chiang, 2003). In his book *A Space for Hate*, Adam Klein (2010) terms such framing as "information laundering" that helps provide an air of legitimacy to the group. The group essentially asserts that it is proclaiming its proud heritage, that this heritage is being "canceled" by the political left, and that they are victims of reverse discrimination. This "soft core" frame may attract individuals who are uneasy about more extreme sites, and possibly serve as gateway for recruitment (vis à vis links to more extreme sites or literature) to maintain engagement with individuals who have "aged out" of in-person participation, and to cultivate quiet sympathizers (Burris, Smith, & Strahm, 2000).

3.3 Contextual and Society-Level Factors

The role of prejudiced individuals or intergroup threat notwithstanding, hate speech does not operate in a vacuum. Broader societal and contextual factors also play a role in the expression of hate speech. To illustrate the interplay of these different levels of analysis, consider an analogy from the potential causes of gun violence: At the individual level, there is a person who pulls the trigger, and that particular person might be especially volatile or have nominal regard for the lives of others. At the group level, potential causes might derive from intergroup hatred based on symbolic differences or from rival gangs in genuine conflict over territory. The broader context in which gun violence occurs includes the ease of acquiring guns by theft or purchase, is manifest where industries and constituencies directly or indirectly benefit from gun availability, and contains a criminal justice system that may (or may not) have capacity or desire to address violence. In like fashion, broader contextual factors may fail to constrain hate speech and may even perpetuate it. Individual differences in prejudice or experience of intergroup threat might potentiate hate speech, but the broader context facilitates (or inhibits) its reach and spread. These include systemic factors that maintain the status of historically powerful groups as well as ordinances and laws that tolerate (or attempt to limit) hate speech.

In her book *Hate Speech* (2021), Caitlin Carlson argues that hate speech is a structural phenomenon insofar as it allows groups in power to maintain their privileged position. And, indeed, hate speech can maintain the status hierarchy by threatening people from marginalized groups into submission or withdrawal (Gelber & McNamara, 2016). In extreme cases, hate speech also legitimizes extreme negative behavior toward out-groups such as genocide and curtailed immigration (Blum et al., 2007; Esses, Medianu, & Lawson, 2013). But if privileged position provides context for the perpetuation of hate speech, one needs to consider the historical and systemic factors that perpetuate privilege and maintain inequity in the first place. Urban ecosystems, for example, perpetuate inequity (Schell et al., 2020). Schell and colleagues note that government-sponsored policies of the past stratified neighborhoods by race and/or economic status (e.g., US redlining policies through 1968, which denied Black families housing in certain neighborhoods). Today, the still-primarily, White neighborhoods are spared dangerous environmental legacies such as urban heat islands, limited green space, and polluting industries while enjoying better access to health care and healthy food options. In short, members of powerful groups benefit from inequity *even when they are not actively working to create it*. Critical race theory (Delgado & Stefancic, 2023) makes this point even more pointedly: *"Because racism advances the interests of both white elites (materially) and working-class whites (psychically), large segments of society have little incentive to eradicate it"* (p. 9). By extension, even if many individuals from powerful groups neither use nor encourage hate speech themselves, they have little incentive to eradicate it from society when it helps to preserve their privileged position.

People from powerful groups not only have little incentive to mitigate systemic factors that underlie group disparities but they also may be unlikely to recognize such factors. White Americans, for example, tend to understand racism less in terms of systemic institutional practices and more in terms of the intentional acts of prejudiced individuals (e.g., Adams, O'Brien, & Nelson, 2006; O'Brien et al., 2009; Schaeffer & Edwards, 2022); men similarly may be less sensitive to institutional reasons for sexism than to individualized causes (Blodorn, O'Brien, & Kordys, 2010). By extension, calling out specific hate speech episodes may perpetuate the individualized view of racism, and ignore how those racist expressions reflect an underlying ideology (Bouvier & Machin, 2021). Reduced sensitivity to systemic factors in part may stem from motivation to believe that the status quo hierarchy derives from individual merit; for example, stronger meritocracy beliefs among White Americans predict the endorsement of individual-level explanations of racism for negative events associated with Hurricane Katrina (O'Brien et al., 2009). Powerful groups' reduced sensitivity to systemic racism also might derive from limited knowledge about historical incidents related to discrimination against less powerful groups. White Americans, for example, have less accurate knowledge about anti-Black racist events than do Black Americans; less accurate knowledge predicts blunted perceptions of racism (Nelson, Adams, & Salter, 2012). What knowledge people acquire can be affected at the system level, through legislation and educational policies. Contemporarily, for example, there are some legislative efforts that actively seek to "white-wash" US history which, eventually, will affect the knowledge that some young people acquire. Florida, for example, has enacted a curriculum that distorts and omits critical events in Black US history (e.g.,the 2023 Florida curriculum, Ellis, 2023; for a broader discussion, see Reyna, Bellovary, & Harris, 2022). California, to contrast, recently *prohibited* schools from banning textbooks that include the contributions of people of color, consider gender diversity, and discuss sexual orientation (AP, September 26, 2023). Over time, one might expect further decline in White Americans' recognition of racism and hate speech in Florida relative to California, as a function of their school ecosystem and larger societal macrosystem.

So, to the extent that there are systemic or institutional structures that encourage (or fail to discourage) hate speech, people from powerful groups likely benefit from those structures, have little incentive to disband those structures even if they do not benefit (i.e., there is no reason to change status quo), and may not even perceive those structures as supporting hate speech. The most obvious structures that effectively allow or attempt to restrict hate speech are statements regarding freedom of expression and speech codes. The First Amendment of the United States Constitution guarantees the right of free speech, which technically includes hate speech. Exceptions include speech that involves perjury, disrupts government function, and "fighting words." "Fighting words" are understood to be those that incite immediate breach of peace, are intended to be hurtful, and that the audience cannot avoid. Hate speech that comprises inflammatory face-to-face slurs thus may not be protected under the First Amendment (e.g., *Chaplinsky* v. *New Hampshire* 1942), whereas the distribution of inflammatory pamphlets that one is not forced to read might be protected (e.g., *Beauharnais* v. *Illinois* 1952). A good deal of anonymous hate speech can thrive as free speech in virtual environments, insofar as targets are not forced to read or react to it, and consequently may be difficult to parse as a "true threat" to the immediate peace (Woods & Ruscher, 2021b). A jealously guarded right of free expression carries with it the cost of tolerating many forms of hate speech.

While constitutional scholars and the courts wrestle with free speech restrictions, ordinary citizens have subjective perceptions of what free speech means … and sometimes their perceptions are applied strategically. Notably, White and Crandall (2017) showed that individuals who were higher in anti-Black prejudice perceived greater violation of free speech rights when White students were expelled after singing racially charged songs. Perhaps more telling, White and Crandall also showed that individuals high in anti-Black prejudice invoked free speech more strongly for an anti-Black Facebook post than for an anti-police force posting. Thus, people sometimes invoke free speech selectively – when it maintains the privileged position of their groups – rather than as a general principle. Conceptually replicating and extending White and Crandall (2017), Roussos and Dovidio (2018) also found, relative to participants lower in anti-Black bias, that participants higher in anti-Black bias tended to view a White person writing a racist note as exercising his free speech. The White person had written *"Get out of here, [n-word]*," and also made a symbol-based threat (e.g., hanging an effigy in the park or placing a burning effigy on the target's lawn). Participants' free speech beliefs predicted whether placing the effigy was perceived as a hate crime. Investigating a relation between hate speech and hate crime is important, insofar as prosecution of hate crime often requires demonstration that the perpetrator explicitly held negative group-based views (see also Roussos & Dovidio, 2019). But again, legality notwithstanding, the societal value of free speech is a backdrop against which hate speech exists, and people may invoke that value strategically.

Although some forms of hate speech are tolerated as freedom of expression, some local entities have tried to curtail its expression. Campus speech codes that are prevalent in higher education settings are notable examples. Between 1970 and 2000, the population of US college students increasingly became less tolerant of racist speakers or teachers (Chong, 2006), and universities continually endeavored to craft codes aligned with student sentiments without violating free speech rights. Speech codes, along with diversity–equity–inclusion (DEI) initiatives in general, may signal low tolerance for hate speech on college campuses, but the codes themselves sometimes have been ruled unconstitutional. For example, a University of Wisconsin code prohibited "discriminatory comments," but was ruled as too vague and as not limited to expressions that incite immediate breach of the peace (i.e., fighting words; for additional examples, see Heumann & Church, 1997). College students' intolerance of prejudiced speech during the latter part of the twentieth century foreshadowed their contemporary twenty-first century protests to high-profile ultraconservative speakers (e.g., Milo Yiannopoulos) in the decades that followed (CBS News, 2018; Simonton, 2018). Similarly, in the UK, university speakers are disinvited as a preemptive silencing strategy or are shouted down through inhibitory silencing (Malcolm, 2021). At the contextual level, these tensions are manifesting as universities' efforts to balance free speech with respect for persons, students' frustrations that the scales appear tipped toward allowing hateful speech, and national-level conversations about the ongoing controversy of free speech in higher education (For a US-focused discussion, see Brown, 2017; for discussion of related issues in the UK, see Anthony, 2016).

University settings notwithstanding, people in the United States on the whole are more tolerant of group-offensive speech than are people from other nations and also are less supportive of restrictions against hate speech (Pew Research Center, 2016). Other nations and international entities also value freedom of speech, but their official condemnation of hate speech is arguably stronger than what is seen in the US Constitution. For example, Article 4 of the International Convention for the Elimination of All Forms of Racial Discrimination (1969) reads that its parties "shall declare an offence *punishable by law all dissemination of ideas based on racial superiority or hatred*, incitement to racial discrimination, as well as all acts of violence or incitement to such acts against any race or group of persons of another colour or ethnic origin, and also the provision of any assistance to racist activities, including the financing thereof" [italics added]. Note that the expression of racial superiority or hatred – even in the absence of incitement of violence – is stated as unacceptable. More recently, the Council of Europe Committee of Ministers (1997) recommended prohibition of hate speech from public authorities:

> The governments of the member states, public authorities and public institutions at the national, regional and local levels, as well as officials, have a special responsibility to refrain from statements, in particular to the media, which may reasonably be understood as hate speech, or as speech likely to produce the effect of legitimising, spreading or promoting racial hatred, xenophobia, anti-Semitism or other forms of discrimination or hatred based on intolerance. *Such statements should be prohibited and publicly disavowed whenever they occur* [Principle 1, italics added].

The prosecution of European public officials for hate speech underscores presence of this broader social context (e.g., see Pettersson, 2019 for a discussion of cases in Finland; see Jacobs & van Spanje, 2021 for discussion of the Netherlands).

Whether formal injunctions against hate speech are supported, proposed, enforced, or ignored depends significantly upon communities and institutions. Indeed, injunctions that are perceived as nonlegitimate restrictions on freedom can cause psychological reactance, and prompt the very opposite of the desired behavior (Sittenthaler, Steindl, & Jonas, 2015). Communities and institutions can vary dramatically with respect to their *climates* for following formal and informal injunctions and prescriptions. Climates are shared understandings of norms, formal and informal policies, and practices; in work organizations, for example, there can be safety climates and service climates, as well as toxic climates that tolerate (or encourage) bullying, harassment, or incivility (Priesemuth & Schminke, 2024). When organizational climates tolerate incivility – rude behavior that is ambiguous with respect to harmful intent – that incivility is likely to be directed toward employees who are underrepresented with respect to gender or race (Cortina et al., 2011). Women of color are particularly likely to experience incivility at work (Cortina et al., 2011) as were Chinese workers in the United States and Canada in the early months of the COVID-19 pandemic (Shen et al., 2024). Although incivility may or may not include blatant hate speech (e.g., face-to-face derogatory slurs), uncivil climates are dismissive of microaggressions such as overheard derogatory remarks and jokes, encourage reinterpretation of a perpetrator's remarks as not intending harm, or provide half-hearted support or even discouragement for reporting discrimination. Organizational climates also can vary with respect to justice (e.g., whether decisions are fair, adhere to policies, are explained appropriately, communicated with respect) as well as climate for tolerance for sexual harassment; these climate variables impact the prevalence of sexual harassment – including sexist and sexually hostile communications – in the US military (Rubino et al., 2018). At the broader level of region or nation, climates can be more or less tolerant of discrimination. For example, Sarrasin and colleagues (Sarrasin et al., 2012) examined the relation between ideological climate across Swiss municipalities and citizens' opposition to antiracism laws. Even after statistically controlling for individual-level predictors such as income and political orientation, opposition to antiracism laws was greatest in conservative municipalities.

By extension, one would expect hate speech to be tolerated most in regions or nations with conservative ideologies, organizations with incivility climates, or countries with high levels of prejudice against particular groups. For example, in a study across nineteen countries, Glick and colleagues (Glick et al., 2000) linked national levels of ambivalent sexism (both hostile and benevolent) with indices of equality that include percentage of women in politics, management positions, and shared income. Given that several studies (e.g., Cralley & Ruscher, 2005; Douglas & Sutton, 2014; Tipler & Ruscher, 2019) link individuals' level of sexism with sexist language, one expects that hate speech toward women would be tolerated where national levels of sexism are high. In addition, high national levels of benevolent sexism likely predict anti-trans legislation and hate speech toward transgender people, to the extent that anti-trans rhetoric often is couched as assuring fairness in women's/girls' sports and protecting women/girls in bathrooms (Atwood, Morgenroth, & Olson, 2024). National conversations about laws, rights, threats, politics, sports, and entertainment create the contextual backdrop in which hate speech is curbed or thrives; consideration of all of them is well beyond the scope of the current work.

Fortunately, organizational climates also can reflect prosocial and positive qualities. Just as there are climates for safety and service, there also are climates for diversity. Diversity climates express values around diversity, equity, and inclusion (DEI) and, when supported with evidence, can successfully attract minority members (Ragland & Sommers, 2024) and provide safety cues to current members (Chaney, Sanchez, & Remedios, 2016). For example, the presence of diversity awards signals reduced threats to stigmatized identity for White women and for men of color (Chaney, Sanchez, & Remedios, 2016). One might expect that a diversity climate not only inhibits hateful speech from current community members but also suppresses interest of potential new members who are high in motivations to express their prejudices.

3.4 Summary

Like most complex phenomena, the factors that encourage the production and tolerance of hate speech are multifaceted with respect to level and relevant mechanisms. Individuals differ with respect to how strongly they hold prejudices against target groups, their general desire to maintain hegemony in society, and how willing they are to openly express bias and hatred. At the group level, realistic threats to physical well-being and competition for resources can perpetuate hatred and contempt, as can symbolic threats to worldview, avowed religious certainties, and jealously guarded cultural preferences. Threatened individuals are situated in a larger ecology that may foster an uncivil climate, be stubbornly ignorant of systemic bias, or support laws or codes that tolerate hate speech. Some thematic features may cut across levels of analysis. For example, the motivation to maintain hegemony is seen at the individual (e.g., SDO), group (e.g., a dominant group's response to symbolic or realistic threat), and societal/contextual levels (e.g., systemic racism and sexism). Alternatively, the theme of emotional animosity recurs at the individual (e.g., anger or anger proneness), group (e.g., negative intergroup emotions exacerbated by threat), and societal levels (e.g., subcultures such as hate groups that foment anger and aggression). Regardless of the factors underlying it or the level of analysis used to consider those factors, hate speech has negative consequences for targets, casual observers, and society as a whole. The next section discusses these consequences.

4 Consequences of Hate Speech

Targets of hate speech report that their feelings or concerns often are invalidated or dismissed (e.g., Harwood et al., 2012; Johnson et al., 2021; Sue et al., 2019). A nontarget may tell recipients of hate speech that they are too sensitive or that they misunderstood others' intentions. After all, it's only words (and symbols, and slurs, and dehumanization). A consistent body of literature attests that targets are objectively harmed by hate speech: They experience anxiety, depressed affect, and silencing. Words wound. Moreover, observers are not immune to the effects of hate speech. Hate speech can elicit stereotypes. It can normalize the subsequent use and tolerance of hate speech, fostering an increasingly hostile society. Indeed, burgeoning empirical evidence links hate speech with violence.

4.1 Effects on Targets

Experiencing hate speech is a relatively common occurrence for people who belong to groups that historically have held limited power. In a community and university sample comprising people of color, racially-based hate speech was reported by 46 percent of women and 68 percent of men (Cowan & Hodge, 1996); similar estimates in a community sample reported that 46 percent experience racially offensive speech on a daily basis (Nielsen, 2002). Gender-based hate speech was also reported as a frequent and regular occurrence (Cowan & Hodge, 1996; Nielsen, 2002). In a more recent study, African American adults reported online racism (e.g., receiving racist memes and posts; encountering racist materials) as relatively common (i.e., averaging 3.10, on a 5-point scale from never to always; Cavalhieri et al., 2024). Beyond race, a study by the Pew Research Center indicated that over 50 percent of American LGBT adults report being subjected to slurs or jokes focused on their sexual orientation or gender identity (Pew Research Center, 2013). Hate speech exposure among children and adolescents in online settings similarly is high, ranging from 31.4 percent to 68.5 percent reported across various studies (Kansok-Dusche et al., 2022); in their systematic review, Kansok-Dusche et al. note that most prevalence data are based on self-reports of incidence and frequency of exposure. In short, experiencing hate speech is hardly a rarity, so its potential harms warrant attention.

By definition, hate speech is directed at social identity. Targeting social identity is quite different from an individualized insult. For example, a Black man who has been called the "N-word" has a very different experience than a Black man who has been called a "f–ing a–hole." First, in the broadest sense, the experience of having one's social identity assaulted by hate speech is traumatic, and follows typical stages of traumatic exposure (Leets, 2002). The stages comprise the immediate impact of disorganization (e.g., shock, disbelief, feeling violated), followed by emotional swings (e.g., fear, loss of trust, assaulted dignity), followed finally by coping efforts (e.g., vigilance, attitude revision). Second, the racial slur may involve historical and intergenerational trauma: The "N-word" evokes centuries of historical racial trauma experienced by Black people who were enslaved and colonialized. Racial trauma carries psychological effects such as post-traumatic stress symptoms and flashbacks, as well as the historical trauma of enslavement and genocide (Comas-Díaz, Hall, & Neville, 2019). Historical trauma is intergenerational, as the fears, stories, and coping strategies pass from older adults to younger people in identity groups such as racial or ethnic groups (e.g., Frankish & Bradbury, 2012). Historical trauma, as well as stories of resilience, also can pass across generations of sexual minority groups (e.g., Bower et al., 2021). Thus, hate speech is powerful in part because it reassaults existing wounds.

Moreover, because hate speech is directed at the identity *group*, an assault against one member is an assault against all. People who share an assaulted person's identity can be traumatized by hearing about hate crimes (i.e., secondary exposure; Bor et al., 2018; Paterson, Brown, & Walters, 2019), and it is reasonable to infer that secondary exposure to hate speech has similar negative consequences. Finally, hate speech is an assault against a social identity with whom people may have the strongest ties – family and family-by-choice, friends, members of a faith community. Targets may be torn about disclosing the experience to their social support network because they want to protect others from the traumatic experience. Unfortunately, not disclosing a discrimination event is a form of avoidant coping, which typically is associated with negative consequences (Jacob et al., 2023).

Like revictimization and polyvictimization in other domains (e.g., Charak et al., 2020; Turner et al., 2016), assaults from hate speech likely are repetitive and cumulative. In a study about online gaming by men of color, Ortiz (2019) notes that gamers report that racist comments are common (e.g., *"I've been called spic and wetback so many times, I couldn't point out one specific time."*). Research in the related area of bullying reveals that ethnic minority youth who report bullying and racial discrimination in one arena (e.g., face-to-face victimization) are increasingly likely to report concurrent bullying and racial discrimination in another arena (e.g., cyberbullying; Weinstein, Jensen, & Tynes, 2021). As with cyberbullying, the expected severity of face-to-face versus digital harassment may depend upon a complex interaction of gender, nationality, and publicness (M. F. Wright et al., 2021).

Although the cumulative and pervasive experience of hate speech may render it difficult to parse which medium or particular incident is driving long-term negative consequences for a hate speech target, diary methods might be used to examine day-to-day fluctuations in anxiety and health-relevant outcomes. For example, Flanders (2015) examined microaggressions – including exposure to slurs and prejudiced comments – reported by emerging adults who identified as bisexual across thirty days; microaggressions were associated with increased anxiety. Similarly, Ong and colleagues (Ong et al., 2017) examined how reported microaggressions – including racist comments about Asian Americans – impacted sleep quality reported the following day in a fourteen-day diary study of Asian American college students. Daily diary research focused specifically on the experience of hate speech, in its many forms, could assess both the cumulative and temporal impacts of hate speech on targets.

The potential harm of hate speech to targets also may be magnified because sources often are nonobvious or anonymous. Many prototypic examples of hate speech such as face-to-face racial slurs are attributable to a discrete source or organization. In such cases, targets can identify who poses the immediate threat to their group, even if the source is not punished. In contrast, it may not be immediately evident who generated racist graffiti, posted an anonymous online comment, erected a burning cross, or slid a group-targeting note under one's door. This heightened uncertainty about the threat source can perpetuate anxiety and create a feedback loop of anxiety and hypervigilance (Grupe & Nitschke, 2013). For example, because of the uncertainty it creates, anonymous hate speech may induce effects such as cognitive depletion. Cognitive depletion in intergroup settings can occur when targets allocate portions of their cognitive resources to worrying about nontargets' intentions, rather than focusing on whatever the task at hand might be. For example, Murphy et al. (2012) found that Black people who interacted with a White person who was subtly – but not blatantly – biased later evinced poor performance on a cognitive task. Faced with a known source who is blatantly biased, targets know where they stand, whereas faced with subtle bias, targets waste precious cognitive resources ascertaining a source's intentions and beliefs. Anonymous sources likely mimic these subtle or ambiguously biased sources. Thus, the uncertain identity of the threat source – anonymity – likely adds to the harm of the hate speech event itself (Woods & Ruscher, 2021b).

An anonymous message also obviates how widely held the prejudiced attitude might be within the local environment. Is the offending source a single individual or a group? Does the messaging reflect widely held attitudes of the powerful group, does it reflect the secret views of people who on the surface seem nonthreatening, or does it only reflect a fringe subgroup in the local environment? When hate speech comes from multiple sources (e.g., several internet commenters), emotional distress experienced by targets can be magnified (Lee-Won et al., 2020), so it matters whether the anonymous message seems to represent multiple voices. Even if the targeted group infers that members of the powerful group may not *commit* acts of violence or actively discriminate, they may infer sins of *omission*: The targeted group is deemed too unimportant to bother removing abusive internet posts or offensive graffiti (cf. Wilson, 2014). Inaction reflects tacit agreement, absence of disagreement, or apathy. While not the commission of hate speech per se, inaction may foster an environment where explicit acts of hate speech are tolerated. Ultimately, to the extent that targets infer that offensive messaging reflects a widely held community belief, targets may presume that the immediate environment is hostile and unsafe (cf. Woods & Ruscher, 2024). Hostile social (Kneale & Bécares, 2023) or work (Cortina et al., 2011) environments are associated with negative outcomes for members of historically underrepresented groups. To the extent that targeted individuals believe that hateful messaging – and a failure to address it – reflects the views of a more powerful group, anxiety and dread may be self-perpetuating.

Research generally supports the idea that hate speech produces consequential harms such as depression, fear, and anxiety. For example, Gelber and McNamara's (2016; p. 333) interviews with minority and indigenous communities in Australia include poignant accounts about hate speech such as:

> *"It was like crushing emotionally and spiritually. And physically."*

> *"You can never, you can never repair damage in that content once it's been put out there. It lingers, it stays, it smells, it hangs around."*

> *"Our kids also feel hopeless and ask why their parents as Muslims are doing something wrong."*

The qualitative data underscore hate speech as an oppressive and pervasive stressor, and also illustrate the shared pain when social identity is assaulted. The metaphoric language is particularly apt at capturing depressed affect. Being pushed downward (i.e., crushing) and irreparable harm (i.e., lingering damage) both evoke depression and hopelessness. A more recent qualitative study similarly observed that exposure to racially offensive online posts made Black university students question their worth and potential (Hurd et al., 2022).

Quantitative studies also point to negative consequences relevant to depression, hopelessness, fear, and anxiety. For example, Schneider, Hitlan, and Radhakrishnan (2000) observed that the combination of verbal harassment and work exclusion predicted symptoms of post-traumatic stress (PTS) disorder among Latino personnel in a large southwestern school district. Similarly, among African American individuals, online racism predicts psychological distress to a similar degree as does institutional racism (Cavalhieri et al., 2024). In a notable example focused on hate speech in particular, Wypych and

Bilewicz (2024) examined the relation between frequent exposure to hate speech, symptoms of depression, and PTSD in over 700 Ukrainian migrants living in Poland. Hate speech affected depression through acculturation stress (e.g., stress from language challenges or cross-cultural differences) and affected PTS symptoms partially through acculturation stress. Similarly, psychological distress, including anxiety and depression, is predicted by the degree of exposure to racist commentary during online gaming among Black emerging adults (Keum & Hearns, 2022). Finally, using a very different methodology, Mullen and Smyth (2004) relied upon archival data to examine the link between ethnic epithets and suicide rates. They found that the number of negative epithets that were used to describe immigrant groups in the United States predicted suicide rates. This remained true even after the authors statistically controlled for the suicide rates in each ethnic group's country of origin. Insofar as immigrant groups are aware of the epithets that are directed at them (Rice et al., 2010), the overall prevalence of negative epithets serves well as a group-level proxy for exposure to hate speech as well as a recognized signal of threat in the social environment. As a whole, converging evidence across a variety of samples and methodologies thus supports a rather consistent link between hate speech and targets' psychological distress.

Hate speech also may produce harms that essentially silence the target, restrict freedom of movement, and violate dignity (Gelber & McNamara, 2016). This type of harm essentially involves the free speech of one group silencing the free speech of another group (for a discussion, see Levin, 2010 chapter 4). Matsuda and colleagues (Matsuda et al., 1993) report that targets' dominant response to hate speech is silence and withdrawal. That observation is born out in later empirical studies. For example, in a study of college students who identified as Jewish or as homosexual, Leets (2002) reported that the most common response to hate speech was withdrawal or passive response. More recently, a qualitative study of verbal microaggressions in a college residence hall showed similar responses of withdrawal or avoiding confrontation (Harwood et al., 2012; p. 165). Students of color were reported as saying:

> *"I didn't want to start any drama within the hall, so I didn't say anything."*

> *"I'll just leave it along because there's no point in getting into an argument over something we can just leave alone."*

The tendency to withdraw in the face of hate speech is a strategy for avoiding additional harm. People avoid retaliating against powerful provocateurs because retaliating against someone who holds more power is risky (O'Neal & Taylor, 1989). Ironically, because the failure to retaliate produces no apparent threat to the peace (i.e., the "fighting words" feature), onlookers may not recognize the negative effects of hate speech on targets. In fact, third-party observers often interpret a nonresponse to mean that little harm has been done (Cowan & Mettrick, 2002). The cumulative effect of perpetually silencing targets and repressing target actions has been understood as a constitutive harm of hate speech (i.e., that hate speech constitutes a harm in and of itself, even in advance of downstream consequential harms). Theorists argue that hate speech silences, subordinates, prompts avoidance from social and physical spaces, and perpetuates structural power differences (Levin, 2010; Matsuda et al., 1993; Woods & Ruscher, 2021b). Because failure to act, speak up, or occupy spaces comprise "negative symptoms" that are indirect and cumulative, the constitutive harm of hate speech may not be easily recognized, particularly by members of historically powerful groups.

But as individuals or as groups, rather than withdrawing from the situation, targets sometimes stand up to hate speech and other discriminatory actions. Targets may confront specific speakers. In the Leets (2002) study reported earlier in this section, the second most common response to hate speech among Jewish or homosexual participants was an assertive response, such as telling the speaker that they had acted inappropriately or asking the speaker to apologize. Similarly, Swim and Hyers (1999) found that 45 percent of women confronted a sexist remark, typically by correcting or questioning the speaker (e.g., "*What did you just say?*"). More broadly, exposure to hate speech and other discriminatory actions may prompt activism. Szymanski and Lewis (2015) showed that race-related stress (which included hate speech and discriminatory language) predicted Black individuals' participation in demonstrations, antiracism events, and other activist activities. In the academic arena, scholars of color and their allies also may criticize apparent tolerance for speakers who assault the dignity of underrepresented groups, and question the validity of free speech justifications. And, in the public arena, celebrity activists may call out White supremacy – in which hate speech plays a part – through demonstrations at sporting events (see Chaplin & Montez de Oca, 2019 for a discussion), through music lyrics (e.g., Stanford, 2011) or on social media (e.g., Harlow & Benbrook, 2019). This very public counterspeech conceivably is instrumental in communicating that hate speech sand discriminatory language are unacceptable (e.g., campus codes of conduct that condemn hate speech, renaming places that commemorate prejudiced historical figures, removing stereotypically offensive mascots and advertising icons). Such pressure on donors and financial sponsors ultimately can effect change (e.g., pressure by major stadium sponsor FedEx to rename the *Washington Redskins*, Sharrow, Tarsi, & Nteta, 2021).

4.2 Effects on Nontargets

Although hate speech may be directed at members of a targeted group, it also is encountered by nontargets. Some people who experience hate speech are incidental recipients: They see the graffiti, overhear a racial slur, read a dehumanizing headline; these individuals may be uninvolved members of a majority group or allies who are vigilant for the discriminatory behavior of others. Exposing such individuals to hate speech may activate stereotypes, desensitize them to its occurrence, or prompt confrontation and social punishment. Alternatively, some nontargets may be an intended audience of active recipients: They are individuals who potentially share the views of the hate speech perpetrator. Rather than a proverbial dog whistle, hate speech shared with like-minded others is a blaring trumpet that "speaks the quiet part out loud." For these individuals, hate speech constitutes "a call to action" against the targeted identity group.

For observers, hate speech can activate stereotypes. Stereotypes comprise shared generalizations about the traits, behaviors, and other characteristics of people belonging to a particular social category. People vary in the degree to which stereotypes are accessible in their minds; stereotypes may be activated in certain situations (but not others) and may (or may not) be applied in everyday decision-making, judgments, and behavior (for a review, see Fiske, 1998). Stereotypes can be activated by the real or strong symbolic presence of the category, including photographs or group-signifying names (e.g., O'Brien & Merritt, 2022). Insofar as hate speech implies the social category (along with negative connotation), it similarly can activate associated stereotypes and thereby color subsequent judgment. For example, in an early study of derogatory ethnic labels, Greenberg and Pyszczynski (1985) contrived for White students to overhear criticism of a Black student who lost a debate; in some cases, the criticism included an ethnic slur. Compared to participants who heard race-irrelevant criticism or participants who heard no comments, participants exposed to the slur subsequently denigrated the Black student's skill. Later work replicated this effect when the target was a Black defense attorney and additionally showed that the denigration extended to the attorney's White client (Kirkland, Greenberg, & Pyszczynski, 1987). Work nearly a decade later suggested that such racial slurs primarily affect third-party individuals who hold preexisting negative attitudes about the targeted group (Simon & Greenberg, 1996), consistent with findings that individual differences can be an important moderator of the effects of hate speech (e.g., Roussos & Dovidio, 2018; White & Crandall, 2017; see also Fasoli, Maass, & Carnaghi, 2015).

Hate speech also can cause dehumanization by third-party observers and, conversely, dehumanizing metaphors can cause negative attitudes. Fasoli et al. (2016) subliminally primed heterosexual Italian students with either a homophobic epithet, a generic category label for homosexual people, or a category-irrelevant insult, then participants each interacted with a gay male conversation partner. The homophobic epithet increased dehumanization of the conversation partner relative to the other conditions, and also tended to increase the physical distance that they sat from him. From a social cognitive perspective, a homophobic slur activates attributes such as deviance and immorality, which reduces empathy and justifies exclusion from humanity. Consistent with this notion, hate speech may even short-circuit the brain's inclination to respond to other's pain (Pluta et al., 2023). People denigrated with hate speech are not seen as fully human and, consequently, do not warrant empathetic responding. On the converse, dehumanizing metaphors can play a causal role by influencing attitudes. When potential female voters were described with feline predator imagery, participants more strongly endorsed hostile sexism items from the Ambivalent Sexism Inventory (Tipler & Ruscher, 2019). This finding suggests that, like wild animals, women who push assertively into male disciplines must be subdued and restrained. Similarly, when immigrants were depicted through the parasite metaphor, participants reported stronger resource-based anti-immigrant attitudes and beliefs (Tipler, 2016; see also Esses, Medianu, & Lawson, 2013 in Section 2.2). The vermin metaphor implies that immigrants mindlessly devour resources, and consequently are welcome to neither residence nor resources.

While the effects of stereotype activation and priming vis-à-vis hate speech might be short-lived or temporary, frequent exposure to hate speech may have more sustained impacts with respect to desensitization and solidifying norms (Bilewicz & Soral, 2020). When people are desensitized to negative or extreme events, they show reduced emotional and/or physical responses to those events over time: after repeated exposure to cyberbullying (Pabian et al., 2016), media violence (Krahé et al., 2011), and sexual violence (Linz, Donnerstein, & Penrod, 1988). In like fashion, people can become desensitized to hate speech. In a nationwide sample of 682 Polish late adolescents, Soral, Bilewicz, and Winiewski (2018) showed that frequency of exposure to hate speech about Muslims and refugees predicted reduced sensitivity to hate speech (i.e., it was rated as less offensive); reduced sensitivity, in turn, predicted greater prejudice and anti-immigrant attitudes; a smaller experimental study in the same article conceptually replicated these findings with a wider array of out-groups.

Repeated exposure to hate speech also provides cues about what is normative for a particular environment. People rely upon their observations of others' behavior to ascertain what is standard behavior in a situation, such as the formality of clothing, tolerance of rudeness, or the types of people who are (or are not) present. If large numbers of people are engaged in the behavior, the behavior is seen as acceptable and becomes more likely (e.g., cheating, Daumiller & Janke, 2020; littering, Cialdini, Reno, & Kallgren, 1990). In a study concerned with hateful communication specifically (Hsueh, Yogeeswaran, & Malinen, 2015), New Zealand college students read online comments that either supported or disparaged Asian international students (purportedly written by other students), then left their own comments. Students who read disparaging comments subsequently wrote comments that were significantly more negative than the comments of students in the supportive condition. Essentially, students followed the norm created by their alleged peers. Indeed, Twitter users tend to retweet, like, or reply to covert racist or sexist insults, again reflecting the notion that hateful language spreads as it becomes normalized (Inara Rodis, 2021). Bilewicz and Soral (2020) argue that frequently encountering hate speech similarly can create a descriptive norm that engaging in hate speech is a typical practice. They further propose that highly prejudiced individuals who have a large social network of fellow hate speech users will follow that norm; computer simulations of their full model are consistent with this proposition. Presumably, individuals with high levels of prejudice locate environments where they both transmit and receive hate speech, which amplifies their impact on other people while also exacerbating hate speech's impact on them. Consistent with this notion, a temporal analysis of Gab.com finds that users are becoming more hateful at an increased rate over time (i.e., each cohort of new users is more hateful than the last cohort; Mathew et al., 2020). Essentially, as online social networks become echo chambers of shared views, opinions become more polarized (Santos, Lelkes, & Levin, 2021).

Perhaps the most profound impact of hate speech on nontargets involves its capacity to bolster hate groups and to foment violence. Hate group websites provide a largely anonymous method of recruiting like-minded individuals (Klein, 2010). Reyna et al. (2022) argue that White nationalism comprises a mixture of both nostalgia for a White-dominated society of the past and a disparagement of current affairs (which indirectly and directly is blamed on minorities and groups that threaten White hegemony). Analyses of extremist websites are consistent with this assertion, as the varied content appears to mix in-group superiority with out-group disparagement. For example, Gerstenfeld et al. (2003) showed 50 percent of examined hate sites mentioned economic issues, 31.8 percent contained excerpts from supremacist literature (e.g., *Mein*

Kampf) and 49.7 percent included extremist symbols such as swastikas. Many sites further asserted that White supremacists were actually the victims of other groups (e.g., Anti-Defamation League) that were demonizing them for expressing pride in White heritage; the attempt to elicit sympathy for purported reverse discrimination essentially invokes competitive victimhood (Noor et al., 2012). Similarly, McNamee, Peterson, and Peña (2010) find that major online hate group themes comprise education (e.g., reinterpreting history), participation (e.g., promoting involvement), invocation (e.g., in-group superiority and divine authority), and indictment (e.g., out-group blame and demonization). Although Gerstenfeld et al. (2002) noted that relatively few (16.6 percent) sites explicitly call for violence, it is worth noting that hate group sites also use coded language that is not immediately recognizable to outsiders (e.g., 311 for Ku Klux Klan, K being the eleventh letter of the alphabet; RaHoWa!! as the White supremacist battle cry for "Racial Holy War;" Klein, 2010). Fake stories, propaganda, and "reasoned argument" may justify and inspire violence (Klein, 2010). It goes without saying that, once recruited, members may communicate violent intentions through private means not easily accessed by researchers (e.g., incriminating text messages in advance of the January 6 attack on the US Capital, Gallagher, 2022). Hate speech can be used to inspire like-minded others to attack members of identity groups.

Hate-laced rhetoric at the national level can be associated with increased violence. As already noted, politicians' emotional animosity toward out-groups predicts intergroup-relevant violence several months later (cf. Matsumoto, Frank, & Hwang, 2015). Huynh, Raval, and Freeman (2022) found that Asian American adults reported a dramatic increase in racial discrimination after the COVID-19 pandemic began, when expressions such as "China-virus" and "Hong Kong Flu" laced the national rhetoric. More directly, in an archival study demonstrating that hate speech precedes violence, Nugent, Abrams, and Joseph (2022) examined violent rhetoric by US politicians reported in national newspapers between January 2014 and September 2019. The incidence rate of mass shootings increased almost threefold for each 4.5 percent increase in the number of articles with violent political rhetoric; the increase could not be explained by factors such as gross domestic product or new gun purchases. Nugent et al.'s findings admittedly do not show a causal role for hate speech in producing violence. It may well be that hateful discourse is simply an indicator of the animosity that ultimately perpetrates violence. Or it reflects the perceived consensus against an out-group that can lead to discrimination (Smith & Postmes, 2011). But even if it is merely the proverbial canary in the coal mine, the possibility that hate speech precedes violence certainly warrants attention.

4.3 Summary

People who are targeted by hate speech evince increased depression and anxiety. Hate speech assaults their group identities, wounding directly and repeatedly, harming through secondary exposure, and retraumatizing intergenerationally. Hate speech can energize targets to activism, but often successfully prompts fear and withdrawal. Casual observers are not immune to the effects of hate speech, insofar as hate speech can activate stereotypes and prompt dehumanization. Hate speech can become normalized and desensitize observers to its toxicity, essentially becoming a climate that tolerates group-targeting incivility. And for the not-so-casual observers, hate speech recruits like-minded others and foments violence. It's not "only words." Those words have consequences.

5 Mitigation Efforts

Hate speech is a complex phenomenon, rightly considered at multiple levels of analysis and from an interdisciplinary lens. Beyond general strategies to reduce prejudice (e.g., Hsieh, Faulkner, & Wickes, 2022), the extant literature discusses several mitigation strategies that uniquely target hate speech. These strategies rely on computerized strategies, speech codes, and counterspeech, and are discussed in the next section.

5.1 Computer-Based Strategies

Of the 413 hate speech articles reported in Web of Science in 2022, 107 were from areas of computer science. Although the technical aspects of these computerized strategies are beyond the scope and expertise of the current work, the increasing role of computerized detection strategies warrants attention in a discussion of mitigation. Social media provides a ripe environment for hate speech to occur, and its use is extremely prevalent. For example, among US adults, nearly 50 percent report using Instagram and nearly 70 percent report using Facebook (Pew Research Center, 2024). Most of the aforementioned work has examined the efficacy of various strategies in computerized hate speech detection, typically in online spaces (e.g., comment sections of blogs or news articles; social media posts). In their expert review of the strategies, Chhabra and Vishwakarma (2023) note that some computer techniques extract features from a dataset, such as hate words from the lexicon of particular language, emotional sentiments (usually positive or negative), or consider each hate word within the context of a certain number of adjacent words (N-grams). Alternatively, techniques may involve machine-learning algorithms and natural language processing schemes that have been trained on large datasets (e.g., Twitter) and then applied to newly encountered data. The recurring neural network that develops needs to persist across thousands of updates across time, hence the awkward moniker of long short-term memory. Bidirectional long short-term memory deep-based learning models (BiLSTM) can even pick up the intentional misspellings or coded words commonly used on hate sites (e.g., Saleh, Alhothali, & Moria, 2023). Finally, some algorithms can be trained to detect hateful images from memes, and others examining memes can distinguish hateful irony from harmless content (Hermida & Santos, 2023).

A strength of using computerized strategies lies with their ability to detect and mitigate hate speech in high-volume online environments. Even if hate speech is protected as free speech in many instances, laws may prohibit hate speech when it includes incitement to violence (see Section 3.3). Moreover, many online environments have *terms of use* that prohibit hate speech (e.g., *Facebook, Twitter, YouTube*; MacAvaney et al., 2019) and may have policies for removing posts that violate their policy. Given that frequent hate speech can create a descriptive norm for what is typical (e.g., Bilewicz & Soral, 2020), removal of such content conceivably reduces the perception of how normative such expressions are in that setting. Content can be moderated by human individuals or expert groups, by computer-based strategies, or by humans employing the assistance of computer strategies. According to Wang and Kim (2023), there are only a handful of studies about the acceptance of various sorts of moderation, and results are inconsistent across studies with respect to users' perceptions of whether the removal strategy is trustworthy and legitimate. Conceivably, inconsistency in what type of moderation is accepted may derive from a number of factors, such as the type of platform used, which group is being targeted by hate speech, and the explanation for removal. Wang and Kim also suggest that greater acceptance may be evident in future research studies over time, insofar as acceptance of other computer-assistance technologies eventually grows over time. But it also seems possible that fear of artificial intelligence, conspiratorial beliefs, or concerns about bias may affect acceptability. Removal policies and policing that are deemed nonlegitimate may simply redirect users to less public settings or to sites that purport to advocate free speech (Pew Research Center, 2022).

Removal also could be resented as censorship. An ethnographic analysis of the internet subreddit r/FreeSpeech indicates that many users construe free speech in an absolute sense (e.g., it should be free from legal and social consequences), and that includes distaste for censoring hate speech (Goldman-Hasbun, 2023). For example, popular threads during the period of her study included "*How to get rid of the authoritarian censorship laws in the UK*" and "*The strongest weapon against hateful speech is not repression; it is more speech.*" ~ *Barack H. Obama, 2012.* On the whole, these subredditers expressed considerable concern about restricting hate speech through censorship. Censorship need not be absolute, of course, nor entirely "policed" by the website managers. For example, in the arena of online marketing, preestablishing community standards for posts reduces negative tone in users' complaints about a product … essentially prompting self-censorship (Christodoulides, Gerrath, & Siamagka, 2021). Similarly, strong beliefs that fellow online community members will exert informal social control (e.g., "*In general, members of the Internet community voluntarily work together for the maintenance of norms or social rules*") affects intentions not to post race-related hate speech comments (Jung, 2023). Whereas simple removal of posts is a passive strategy to extinguish the behavior of making offensive posts, informal social control actively encourages alternative behaviors instead. Thus, establishing strong community standards against hate speech – encouraging people to self-censor – probably is more effective in the long run than simple removal via computer algorithms.

An alternative to computer-assisted removal of content entirely is for "bots" to respond to online hate speech with messages that are intended to curb future hate speech expression. Hangartner et al. (2021) note that international and nongovernmental organizations (I/NGOs) increasingly use counterspeech in online settings. Counterspeech generally involves alternative narratives that challenge hate speech without being punitive to the speaker, such as providing rationale for responding with empathy for the targeted group. Hangartner et al.'s study investigated the utility of bots in providing counterspeech messages. In their study, human profiles were created for six bots, who periodically tweeted innocuous messages for four weeks to establish them as apparent "users." Then one of these established bots was randomly assigned to respond to a real user's xenophobic or racist tweet with an empathy message (e.g., "*For African Americans, it really hurts to see people use language like this*"), with a warning about the social consequences of the xenophobic/racist tweet (e.g., "*Hey, remember that your friends and family can see this tweet too*"), or with a humorous meme (e.g., an animal engaged in obstructing behavior with the caption "*It's time to stop tweeting.*"). Empathy-based counterspeech increased the odds that the user deleted the original tweet, and tended to reduce the overall volume in xenophobic or prejudiced tweets on the site an additional four weeks later. Although the effects were small, the study demonstrates the utility of using computer-based strategies to reduce the prevalence of online hate speech. That said, one imagines that some users may feel manipulated if they become aware that bots are being utilized in such ways; it remains an empirical question whether awareness of "bot use" influences effectiveness in reducing hate speech.

Although there are ongoing efforts to enhance accuracy of computerized hate speech detection strategies, strategies still may contain biases. The more familiar issue of bias in facial recognition software provides a good analogy. Like computerized hate speech detection, facial recognition software relies on algorithms and machine learning; it is typically more accurate at identifying specific White men than women or people of color (Castelvecchi, 2020). Consequently, in part because of how the algorithms are derived and trained, facial recognition software might "identify" the wrong person of color or woman that the surveillance system is trying to find. Similarly, the strategies for hate speech detection may rely heavily on the dominant language styles of the databases upon which they are trained, and also may reflect the biases of the organizations that adopt particular strategies. For example, Mozafari, Farahbakhsh, and Crespi (2020) note a disparity in classifying hate speech in tweets from groups that favor African American English (AAE) versus tweets from groups that favor Standard American English (SAE). African American English tweets are more likely to be classified as racist, sexist, hateful, or offensive than SAE tweets. Mozafari et al. subsequently instituted a bias alleviation mechanism that successfully reduced that disparity, but did not eliminate it entirely. Similarly, using another computer-based detection strategy (Perspective), Oliva, Antonialli, and Gomes (2021) found higher levels of toxicity in tweets from prominent US drag queens relative to White nationalists; the authors pose that the particular strategy failed to account for the use of "mock impoliteness" that LGBTQ communities sometimes use to proactively cope with hostility. (Indirect speech forms such as irony and sarcasm are often difficult to detect from written language, and "mock impoliteness" similarly conveys more than literal meaning. Conversely, hate groups may use euphemisms that are not easily flagged as hate speech.) Finally, in response to a *USA Today* article that reported uneven removal of Black women's Facebook posts about police violence (Guynn, 2020), Gray and Stein (2021) argue that the removal strategy surveilled and punished Black women. Differential removal of speech from online platforms thus can be a very modern form of bias and system-level discrimination. It is especially troublesome if the removal strategy is classifying nonhateful messages as hateful (e.g., sarcasm), and ultimately silences an identity group, while euphemistic language bent on intimidation slips past detection.

5.2 Speech Codes and Laws, Revisited

Like *terms of use* for online platforms, laws and campus speech codes may attempt to restrict hate speech. Discussion in Section 3.3 regarding societal factors that underly hate speech focused on biased perceptions about free speech, tension between free speech protections versus protecting dignity of groups with historically low power, and variation across nations in tolerance for hate speech. Here the consideration is the effectiveness of laws and codes, when such laws or codes exist.

Condemnation of hate speech (e.g., Article 4 of the International Convention for the Elimination of All Forms of Racial Discrimination, 1969) is interpreted differently across nations, and may or may not prompt creation of civil or criminal laws. Are such laws effective, and in what ways? Gelber and McNamara (2015) provided a case study of hate speech laws being instituted in the states and territories of Australia, and examined five possible consequences of these laws. First, they assessed whether laws reduced the assaults on target dignity and mitigated the risks of discrimination that hate speech perpetuates; their data were inconsistent in this regard: On the one hand, formal complaints decreased after legislation, but on the other hand, there was high bar for complaints to move forward (e.g., complaints needed to be made by members of the targeted group not by advocates and allies) and targeted groups still reported high levels of verbal abuse through nonformal mechanisms. Second, Gelber and McNamara assessed whether public discourse had become less prejudiced following law inception, by examining letters to newspaper editors; they found that the proportion of prejudiced letters decreased over time (which admittedly may reflect both editors' decision to publish a letter and the writers' biases). Third, they raised the question whether the mere presence of the laws showed symbolic support for targeted communities; interview data with underrepresented minority groups suggested some success in this regard. Fourth, they questioned whether the laws had a chilling effect on open discussion; they found that prejudiced expression was relatively stable across time (although which group was targeted with hateful comments varied). Finally, they raised the possibility of violators being seen as martyrs for free speech and right-wing ideology; at least in their data, prosecutions in Australia were too rare to support this possibility (but see Pettersson, 2019). In sum, at least in this particular case, laws may reduce hate speech in trackable settings (e.g., complaints, letters) but not necessarily in less observable daily life. There was some evidence of a symbolic benefit, although purely symbolic gestures devoid of tangible action may ultimately erode confidence.

With respect to hate speech on college campuses, current literature and public discourse appears focused primarily on free speech, such as whether universities should curtail invitations to high-profile conservative speakers whose presence might elicit unruly demonstrations (see also Section 3.3). An alternative question is how well university leadership, professors, and students are prepared to be critical but civil in addressing multiple positions on controversial topics. Ceci and Williams (2018), for example, suggest that rather than summarily rejecting speakers and topics, university communities need to recognize their own potential for bias (e.g., confirmatory bias; in-group bias) and to become informed about controversial topics. But when free speech values are more salient than values of equality, perceivers are less sensitive to the potential harms of hate speech (Cowan et al., 2002). In that vein, Moses (2021) argues that universities are not obligated to provide forums for viewpoints that are indefensible or obviously untrue. She proposes that campus leaders should consider whether speakers and their positions assault people's dignity, encourage meaningful discussion, and are reasonable based on current scientific knowledge and democratic principles. One imagines that although Moses' position may run afoul of strict free speech advocates, it resonates with DEI initiatives on many university campuses. An invitation to speak at a university arguably signals that a speaker contributes to education and reflects institutional values, so campus community objections to speakers with a history of even thinly veiled hate speech is not surprising.

But campus speech codes also endeavor to modify expression of hate speech among the campus community of students, faculty, and staff. For example, in the United States, protection from discrimination and harassment are provided by applicable federal laws such as Titles VI and VII of the Civil Rights Act of 1964 and Title IX of the Education Amendments of 1972 if federal funds support the institution; hate speech may co-occur with unlawful discriminatory behavior against protected groups. Notably, though, laws do not protect all social groups that experience discrimination (e.g., there currently are no US laws protecting transgender individuals while the Equality Act 2010 does so in the UK). The US federal laws also focus primarily on the severe or sustained harassment that creates a hostile environment. In contrast, hate speech often takes the form of microaggressions that may be challenging to penalize: Slurs or prejudiced jokes overheard or shouted from a distance, graffiti and anonymous messages, and one-off micro-assaults are not easily addressed through formal complaints. Indeed, there are relatively high levels of discrimination and verbal harassment reported by college-aged individuals (see Section 4.1), but these harms may not be conveyed to appropriate authorities, may not "meet the legal bar," or may be met with skepticism or dismissal. With respect to the latter, targeted individuals who report hate speech may face secondary microaggressions such as gaslighting or victim-blaming, in which their experiences are invalidated, reinterpreted as unintentional, and dismissed (Johnson et al., 2021). Conduct codes and value statements that enjoin a college community to be respectful of others' dignity may express a prescriptive norm, but may backfire if codes and statements exist without bona fide actions that support that prescription (cf. Kafka, 2023). Continued need for improvement is echoed by a recent survey from the National Association of Student Personnel Administrators (Dunlap et al., 2023), which found that both university students and administrators considered some of the most important areas on which universities need to focus are improved accountability for racism incidents and increased educational awareness of racism.

Whether campus conduct codes and value statements are effective in curbing discriminatory behaviors such as hate speech is an empirical question. Relying on participants at a large state university in the United States, Campbell and Brauer (2021) reported that although students from marginalized groups felt less respected than students from majority groups, students from marginalized groups also reported that discriminatory behaviors were perpetrated by about 20 percent of their peers. This raised the possibility that discrimination is not dispersed across a wide array of perpetrators but, instead, is concentrated among a smaller set of perpetrators. In their article, Campbell and Brauer also conducted five subsequent field experiments that examined students' behaviors toward confederates posing as members of various marginalized groups (or of nonmarginalized groups); across those experiments, 5–20 percent of the students evinced negative behavior toward confederates who appeared to belong to a marginalized group. The authors concluded that about 20 percent of the students on that campus were responsible for 80 percent of the experienced discrimination (i.e., following the Pareto Principle). That is, most students overtly behave with the respect for dignity that typically is expressed in college values statements and conduct codes, but a notable portion do not. The authors suggest that, if negative behavior is concentrated rather than dispersed among students, one might question the utility of one-size-fits-all mitigation strategies (e.g., implicit bias training that focuses on all students). Instead, one might consider using more targeted strategies. Targeted strategies include shielding and inoculating targets to prepare for bias and how to safely report bias (cf. McGee & Kruger, 2022; Onyeador, Hudson, & Lewis, 2021). It also may include training nontargets in allyship and bystander intervention (see Section 5.3). The individuals who are not committing acts of hate speech can be trained how to recognize hate speech, that ignoring it contributes to normativity, and how to use counterspeech to undercut hate speech in the long run.

5.3 Confrontation and Counterspeech

Although citizens may influence the creation and amendment of laws through civic engagement, and students may influence how university values statements and conduct codes are enacted on their campuses, individuals have their most immediate impacts in how they address hate speech in their everyday lives. Confrontation may be initiated by targets themselves or by allies, carries both risks and benefits, and may require practice or training. Who confronts and the manner in which a confrontation is made can influence its eventual effectiveness.

As noted in Section 4.1, targets sometimes directly confront people who make prejudiced comments (e.g., Leets, 2002; Swim & Hyers, 1999) and they also may engage in collective activism against discrimination. Potential costs of this strategy are that targets may be viewed as hypersensitive complainers and ultimately not be effective. For example, Gulker, Mark, and Monteith (2013) found that participants from a predominantly White sample perceived a Black author of an anti-racism article to be a complainer and were less accepting of the message than if the author was a White person; although the article implied that they were part of the problem, it was not a direct confrontation. However, in a study that involved a peer's direct written confrontation of participants' own potentially racist judgments, White participants' subsequent stereotypic responses did not depend on whether the confronting peer was a Black or White individual (Czopp, Monteith, & Mark, 2006). It thus remains unclear whether (or when) targets themselves or allies are more effective at confronting prejudice and, by extension, hate speech.

In addition to considering *who* delivers the confrontation, *how* the confrontation is made also warrants attention. First, it perhaps goes without saying that any confrontation is more effective than no confrontation at all (Czopp, Monteith, & Mark, 2006). Observers expect that both private and public confrontation of prejudiced remarks will reduce the expression of prejudiced statements in the future, although private confrontations (i.e., that protect "face") are also presumed to affect personal attitudes (Woods & Ruscher, 2021a). On the whole, confrontations that unequivocally point to the perpetrator as a cause of harm appear to be effective. For example, the empathy-based confrontations that were seen to be effective in online settings (Hangartner et al., 2021) essentially pointed out how the particular user's comments cause harm. Similarly, confrontations that provide perpetrators with concrete evidence that they discriminated against a woman increases concerns about avoiding bias in the future (Parker et al., 2018).

Confronting or engaging in counterspeech carries risk, such as making oneself a target or being accused of excessive political correctness or sensitivity (Nelson, Dunn, & Paradies, 2011). Beyond the complainer risk (e.g., Gulker et al., 2013), people can be punished by exclusion or other punishments when they act counter to a group norm that tolerates or perpetuates prejudiced language. For example, adolescents who read about a peer who was the sole challenger to a group's sharing racist humor expected that peer to experience social exclusion as a consequence of speaking up (Mulvey, Palmer, & Abrams, 2016). Punitive outcomes also are seen in online settings, as young adults who challenge online hate nearly double their odds of becoming targets themselves (Costello, Hawdon, & Ratliff, 2017). Adults also recognize the potential risks of speaking out. For example, working adults may consider it risky to confront racist or sexist remarks of a supervisor (Ashburn-Nardo et al., 2014). In part, the decision to confront prejudiced behavior on behalf of one's self or others involves weighing the potential benefits relative to the potential costs (Good, Moss-Racusin, & Sanchez, 2012).

Risks notwithstanding, Sue and colleagues (Sue et al., 2019) emphasize the important functions of the micro-interventions that include confrontation: Micro-interventions provide a sense of self-efficacy and establish a repertoire of prosocial responses that can reinforce norms of respectful interactions. Such confrontations can model strategies for current bystanders to learn how to intervene, send a message to the perpetrator and silent conspirators that hateful speech is not tolerated, and can show support to targets. Indeed, the actions of bystanders who affirm the confronter's actions can mitigate target's feelings of low safety and belongingness (Hildebrand, Jusuf, & Monteith, 2020). On a related vein, targets may appreciate allies' confrontations on their behalf, particularly if the confronting behavior is authentic and not performative (e.g., Hurd et al., 2022). In one notable study (Chu & Ashburn-Nardo, 2022), Black participants recruited through a crowdsourcing website (CloudResearch) viewed a conversation between two White individuals in which one person made a prejudiced comment (e.g., about hiring; critical race theory). The other White person either failed to confront or confronted the commenter in one of several ways. Any type of confrontation supported Black participants' self-esteem and well-being, although Black participants were suspicious of a confrontation that implied external motivations to avoid appearing prejudiced (i.e., essentially performative to cast the confronter in a positive light). For this study, then, the criterion for ascertaining effectiveness was the mitigation of negative effects on targets (rather than reducing prejudiced beliefs or behaviors of perpetrators).

Targets, allies, and bystanders each may need to develop skills with respect to confrontation and counterspeech. Although acquiring empathy develops negative attitudes about hate speech (Soral, Malinowska, & Bilewicz, 2022; Sue et al., 2019), people often need practice in confronting others. As is true of bystander intervention in other prosocial domains, whether intervention actually occurs depends upon confidence in one's requisite intervention skills. Some organizations use diversity training to help undercut discrimination in general (e.g., Bezrukova et al., 2016), while other organizations specifically focus formal training on confrontation techniques (e.g., Ashburn-Nardo, Morris, & Goodwin, 2008). As described in Ashburn-Nardo, Morris, and Goodwin (2008), trainees might watch a video in which a model confronts a prejudiced comment or might role-play a confrontation scenario to gain practice with different strategies. Elementary school children successfully can be taught to employ strategies to respond to gender-based discrimination (e.g., comments that one gender is superior or should play with particular toys; Lamb et al., 2009). Similarly, Sue et al. (2019) suggest arming potential allies with confronting statements such as "*I don't agree with what you just said*" and "*I know you didn't realize this but that comment you made was demeaning.*" Thus, potential allies can learn to disarm or educate the person making the offensive comment. Sue et al. also note, however, that some confrontation is genuinely dangerous for the target and/or confronter, so it may be necessary to enlist the aid of outside authorities.

In sum, the success of confrontation and counterspeech may be judged in terms of how it supports target well-being (e.g., Chu & Ashburn-Nardo, 2022), reduces subsequent hate speech by the original perpetrator and potential perpetrators in the social environment (e.g., Hangartner et al., 2021), and effects change in perpetrators' prejudices and stereotypes (e.g., Chaney et al., 2021). Success also may be marked by impact on bystanders. Although witnessing a confrontation that is hostile can reduce bystanders' intentions to confront in the future (Martinez et al., 2017), modeling or training (as described above) can be effective in teaching confrontation skills. Along that vein, bystanders who are recruited as an ally are likely to speak up if the confronter points out the illegitimacy of a prejudiced remark (King et al., 2024). Finally, effectiveness may be judged by whether the effects persist over time. Several studies find that the positive effects of confrontation endure beyond the immediate time of the confrontation (Chaney & Sanchez, 2018; Chaney et al., 2021; Hangartner et al., 2021), which suggests that training potential allies and targets to confront may be a worthwhile strategy in reducing hate speech.

5.4 Summary

Computer-based strategies, formal codes of speech conduct, and counterspeech training may mitigate hate speech in some circumstances. Referencing back to factors underlying hate speech (Section 3), it is also possible that unique interventions might differentially focus on individual differences of perpetrators such as their degree of social dominance (e.g., Danso, Sedlovskaya, & Suanda, 2007) or might leverage potential confronters' beliefs that people who express prejudice can change (Rattan & Dweck, 2010). At the group level, cooperative intergroup contact can reduce group antipathy and, subsequently, could reduce negative behaviors such as hate speech (Van Assche et al., 2023). Systemic changes are of course the most challenging, and rely upon civic engagement and commitment to organizational change. Any of these approaches might involve changing behavioral norms (Crandall, Eshleman, & O'Brien, 2002) which, even if prejudice remains, could mitigate negative effects experienced by people targeted by hate speech.

6 Conclusion

This Element was prefaced with five contemporary examples of hate speech: university students' circulation of racist memes, a television personality's rant about immigrants, a police chief's racial expletives, politicians charged with anti-Muslim internet postings, and the chilling racially charged threat to an election worker. Hate speech is transmitted digitally, through mass media, in surveilled group settings, anonymously, and in private. It uses derogatory group slurs, metaphoric language, exaggeration, images, and symbols. It derives from individual bias and animus, realistic and symbolic intergroup threat, and through social systems designed to keep some groups "in their place." Its public expression shows hate speech to be normative in certain settings, and allows like-minded individuals to find an echo chamber for their shared beliefs. And it has real and painful consequences for victims. Real-world contemporary examples are diverse and plentiful. Social science literature provides ways to organize what hate speech looks like, why it occurs, and its deleterious effects. And, gradually, social science is providing insights into how to mitigate the negative effects of hate speech and curb its use. As noted in the opening paragraphs, scholarly work on hate speech is increasing at a rapid pace. Next are a few thoughts about which future directions might be especially fruitful.

First, although the application of artificial intelligence and computer-based strategies to hate speech continues to increase exponentially, it primarily is confined to digital environments. For example, nearly all ninety hits in Web of Science for "artificial intelligence" and "hate speech" rely on digital platforms such as Twitter, Facebook, Reddit, and TikTok (19 March, 2024). Hate speech detection algorithms also could be used on other large corpuses such as political speeches, newspaper editorials, music lyrics, television news transcripts. Hate speech in these corpuses might relate to geographical or sociopolitical features (e.g., voting patterns, Implicit Associations, health indicators, crime statistics). Alternatively, they might examine hypothesized relations within the corpus, as illustrated by the application of computational linguistics to study dehumanization of LGBTQ people in *New York Times* articles (e.g., through vector similarity to terms associated with disgust and/or vermin metaphors; Mendelsohn, Tsvetkov, & Jurafsky, 2020). Hate speech detection algorithms also might provide insight into bias reporting on university campuses (e.g., differential reporting styles of allies versus targets; anonymous versus identified reporters; differential threat levels; patterns across target groups; self-reports versus computer-detected prevalence). For example, disparities between anonymous reporting and actual crime statistics (which are public via the Cleary Act) could provide insight into where intervention training and protections especially are warranted. Although detection algorithms are not perfect, they present clear advantages to research that relies upon big data. Doing so may help allocate resources where they are most needed.

Second, further empirical insight would be welcome into the effectiveness of hate speech laws, codes, norms, and climates. Throughout this review, the importance of formal versus informal enjoinments to refrain from hate speech has been a recurring theme. Social science understanding of hate speech would benefit from empirical work that examines how these formal and informal injunctions interact. Galbiati and colleagues (Galbiati et al., 2021) argue that formal laws shift perceived norms (i.e., because behavior actually changes) and then, because behavior shifts, there is implication of what society values or stigmatizes. They support this claim by demonstrating dramatic shifts in social distancing behavior after Boris Johnson's March 2020 COVID-19 lockdown in the UK. Relative to other countries, perceived descriptive norms changed dramatically in the UK. Moreover, citizens initially did not believe that people *ought* to comply (even though people in fact *were* complying), but this ought-actual gap was reduced over time. Essentially, people came to believe that they *should* behave as people *did* behave, even when sanctions and enforcement were light compared to other countries. Norms may desensitize people to hate speech (e.g., Bilewicz & Soral, 2020) but norms, vis-à-vis formal injunctions, also can undercut it (Christodoulides, Gerrath, & Siamagka, 2021). Empirically supported recommendations on how formal hate speech injunctions can reestablish civil climates would be welcome.

Finally, practicing psychologists likely need renewed and sustained attention to the deleterious effects of hate speech in clinical, school, and organizational settings. The stress of hate speech, and discriminatory behavior as a whole, remains high. For example, the 2023 American Psychological Association survey indicated that Black, Latinx, LGBTQIA American adults, and adults with disabilities cite discrimination as a significant stressor (American Psychological Association, 2023). Similarly, the UK Evidence for Equality National Survey (EVENS) in 2021 revealed that 26.1 percent of ethnic minority people reported group-targeting verbal insults prior to the pandemic (Ellingworth et al., 2023). Hate speech and discrimination are thriving in contemporary society. Creating supports and affinity groups in school and workplace settings are important supports for targets of discrimination (Onyeador, Hudson, & Lewis, 2021). Similarly, there is a need for training and continuing education with therapeutic approaches that mitigate depressive feelings of powerlessness and that concurrently instill adapting coping and empowerment (for a discussion, see Pieterse et al., 2012). As of the time of this writing, there remains much to be done to better understand hate speech, to curb its presence and effects on society, and to support targets who bear the immediate brunt of its harms.

References

Adams, G., O'Brien, L. T., & Nelson, J. C. (2006). Perceptions of racism in Hurricane Katrina: A liberation psychology analysis. *Analyses of Social Issues and Public Policy, 6*, 215–235. https://doi.org/10.1111/J.1530-2415.2006.00112.x.

Ahmed, S. (2022). Disinformation sharing thrives with the fear of missing out among low cognitive news users: A cross-national examination of intentional sharing of deep fakes. *Journal of Broadcasting & Electronic Media, 66*, 89–109. https://doi.org/10.1080/08838151.2022.2034826.

Albarello, F., & Rubini, M. (2018). Linguistic discrimination toward Roma: Can intergroup threat enhance bias? *Journal of Language and Social Psychology, 37*, 350–364. https://doi.org/10.1177/0261927X17725880.

Al-Rawi, A. (2015). Online reactions to the Muhammed cartoons: YouTube and the virtual ummah. *Journal for the Scientific Study of Religion, 54*, 261–276. https://doi.org/10.1111/jssr.12191.

American Psychological Association (2023). Stress in America. www.apa.org/news/press/releases/stress/2023/collective-trauma-recovery.

Amici Curiae Brief in Support of Plaintiff-Appellant's Petition for Rehearing En Banc No. 08–16135-BB John Hithon v. Tyson Foods (2010). http://naacpldf.org/files/case_issue/Hithon%20Brief.pdf.

Anthony, A. (2016, June). Is free speech in British universities under threat. *The Guardian.* www.theguardian.com/world/2016/jan/24/safe-spaces-universities-no-platform-free-speech-rhodes.

Anzani, A., Lindley, L., Tognasso, G., Galupo, M. P., & Prunas, A. (2021). "Being talked to like I was a sex toy, like being transgender was simply for the enjoyment of someone else": Fetishism and sexualization of transgender and nonbinary individuals. *Archives of Sexual Behavior, 50*, 897–911. https://doi.org/10.1007/S10508-021-01935-8.

Ashburn-Nardo, L., Blanchar, J. C., Petersson, J., Morrise, K. A., & Goodwin, S. A. (2014). Do you say something when it's your boss? The role of perpetrator power in prejudice confrontation. *Journal of Social Issues, 70*, 615–636. https://doi.org/10.1111/josi.12082.

Ashburn-Nardo, L., Morris, K. A., & Goodwin, S. A. (2008). The confronting prejudiced responses (CPR) model: Applying CPR in organizations. *Academy of Management Learning & Education, 7*, 332–342. https://doi.org/10.5465/amle.2008.34251671.

Associated Press (September 23, 2023). California Governor Signs Law Barring Schoolbook Bans Based on Racial and LGBTQ Teachings. www.nbcnews.com/nbc-out/out-politics-and-policy/california-governor-signs-law-schoolbook-bans-based-racial-lgbtq-teach-rcna117345.

Atwood, S., Morgenroth, T., & Olson, K. R. (2024). Gender essentialism and benevolent sexism in anti-trans rhetoric. *Social Issues and Policy Review, 18,* 171–193. https://doi.org/10.1111/sipr.12099.

Bacon, A. M., May, J., & Charlesford, J. J. (2021). Understanding public attitudes to hate: Developing and testing a U.K. version of the hate crime beliefs scale. *Journal of Interpersonal Violence, 36,* 13365–13390. https://doi.org/10.1177/0886260520906188.

Bailey, A. H., Dovidio, J. F., & LaFrance, M. (2022). "Master" of none: Institutional language change linked to gender bias. *Journal of Experimental Psychology: Applied, 28,* 237–248. https://doi.org/10.1037/xap0000326.

Balliet, D., Wu, J., & De Dreu, C. K. W. (2014). Ingroup favoritism in cooperation: A meta-analysis. *Psychological Bulletin, 140,* 1556–1581. https://doi.org/10.1037/a0037737.

Bareket, O., & Fiske, S. T. (2023). A systematic review of the ambivalent sexism literature: Hostile sexism protects men's power; benevolent sexism guards traditional gender roles. *Psychological Bulletin, 149,* 637–698. https://doi.org/10.1037/bul0000400.

Beal, D. J., O'Neal, E. C., Ong, J., & Ruscher, J. B. (2000). The ways and means of interracial aggression: Modern racists' use of covert retaliation. *Personality and Social Psychology Bulletin, 26,* 1225–1238. https://doi.org/10.1177/0146167200262005.

Berbrier, M. (2000). The victim ideology of White supremacists and White separatists in the United States. *Sociological Focus, 33,* 175–191. Jstor.org/stable/20832074.

Bettencourt, B. A., Talley, A., Benjamin, A. J., & Valentine, J. (2006). Personality and aggressive behavior under provoking and neutral conditions: A meta-analytic review. *Psychological Bulletin, 132,* 751–777. https://doi.org/10.1037/0033-2909.132.5.751.

Bezrukova, K., Spell, C. S., Perry, J. L., & Jehn, K. A. (2016). A meta-analytical integration over 40 years of research on diversity training evaluation. *Psychological Bulletin, 142,* 1227–1274. https://doi.org/10.1037/bul0000067.

Bianchi, M., Caraghi, A., Piccoli, V., Stragà, M., & Zotti, D. (2019). On the descriptive and expressive function of derogatory group labels: An experimental test. *Journal of Language and Social Psychology, 38,* 756–772. https://doi.org/10.1177/0261927X19867739.

Bigsby, E., Bigman, C. A., & Gonzalez, A. M. (2019). Exemplification theory: A review and meta-analysis of exemplar messages. *Annals of the International Communication Association, 43*, 273–296. https://doi.org/10.1080/23808985.2019.1681930.

Bilewicz, M., & Soral, W. (2020). Hate speech epidemic: The dynamic effects of derogatory language on intergroup relations and political radicalization. *Political Psychology, 41*, 3–33. https://doi.org/10.1111/POPS.12670.

Bilewicz, M., Soral, W., Marchlewska, M., & Winiewski, M. (2017). When authoritarians confront prejudice: Differential effects of SDO and RWA on support for hate-speech prohibition. *Political Psychology, 38*, 87–99. https://doi.org/10.111/POPS.12313.

Blodorn, A., O'Brien, L. T., & Kordys, J. (2010). Responding to sex-based discrimination: Gender differences in perceived discrimination and implications for legal decision-making. *Group Processes and Intergroup Relations, 15*, 291–437. https://doi.org/10.1177/1368430211427172.

Blum, R., Stanton, G. H., Sagi, S., & Richter, E. D. (2007). "Ethnic cleansing" bleaches the atrocities of genocide. *European Journal of Public Health, 18*, 204–209. https://doi.org/10.1093/eurpub/ckm011.

Bor, J., Venkataramani, A. S., Williams, D. R., & Tsai, A. C. (2018). Police killings and their spillover effects on the mental health of Black Americans: A population-based, quasi-experimental study. *Lancet, 392*, 302–310. https://doi.org/10.1016/s0140-6736(18)31130-3.

Bouvier, G., & Machin, D. (2021). What gets lost in Twitter "cancel culture" hashtags? Calling out racists reveals some limitations of social justice campaigns. *Discourse & Society, 32*, 307–327. https://doi.org/10.1177/0957926520977215.

Bower, K. L., Lewis, D. C., Bermúdez, J. M., & Singh, A. A. (2021). Narratives of generativity and resilience among LGBT older adults: Leaving positive legacies despite social stigma and collective trauma. *Journal of Homosexuality, 68*, 23–251. https://doi.org/10.1080/00918369.2019.1648082.

Brown, S. (2017). 4 Highlights from a U.S. Senate Hearing on Campus Free Speech. www.chronicle.com/article/4-Highlights-From-a-US/240400.

Burris, V., Smith, E., & Strahm, A. (2000). White supremacist networks on the internet. *Sociological Focus, 33*, 215–235. Jstor.org/stable/20832076.

Campbell, M. R., & Brauer, M. (2021). Is discrimination widespread? Testing assumptions about bias on a university campus. *Journal of Experimental Psychology: General, 150*, 756–777. https://doi.org/10.1037/xge0000983.

Carlson, C. R. (2021). *Hate speech.* Cambridge, MA: The MIT Press.

Castelvecchi, D. (2020). Beating biometric bias. *Nature, 587,* 347–349. www.nature.com/articles/d41586-020-03186-4.

Cavalhieri, K. E., Greer, T. M., Hawkins, D., et al. (2024). The effects of online and institutional racism on the mental health of African Americans. *Cultural Diversity and Ethnic Minority Psychology, 30,* 476–486. https://doi.org/10.1037/cdp0000585.

CBS News. (2018). A war on words on college campuses. www.cbsnews.com/news/a-war-of-words-on-college-campuses/.

Ceci, S. J., & Williams, W. M. (2018). Who decides what is acceptable speech on campus? Why restricting free speech is not the answer. *Perspectives on Psychological Science, 13,* 299–323. https://doi/org/10.1177/1745691618767324.

Cerase, F. P. (1974). Expectations and reality: A case study of return migration from the United States to southern Italy. *The International Migration Review, 8,* 245–263. Jstor.org/stable/3002783.

Cervone, C., Augoustinos, M., & Maass, A. (2021). The language of derogation and hate: Functions, consequences, and reappropriation. *Journal of Language and Social Psychology, 40,* 80–101. https://doi.org/10.1177/0261927X20967394.

Chaney, K. E., & Sanchez, D. T. (2018). The endurance of interpersonal confrontations as a prejudice reduction strategy. *Personality and Social Psychology Bulletin, 44,* 418–429. https://doi.org/10.1177/0146167217741344.

Chaney, K. E., Sanchez, D. T., Alt, N. P., & Shih, M. J. (2021). The breadth of confrontations as a prejudice reduction strategy. *Social Psychological and Personality Science, 12,* 314–322. https://doi.org/10.1177/1948550620919318.

Chaney, K. E., Sanchez, D. T., & Remedios, J. D. (2016). Organizational identity safety cue transfers. *Personality and Social Psychology Bulletin, 42,* 1564–1576. https://doi.org/10.1177/0146167216665096.

Chaplin, K. S., & Montez de Oca, J. (2019). Avoiding the issue: University students' responses to NFL players national anthem protests. *Sociology of Sport Journal, 36,* 12–21. https://doi.org/10.1123/ssj.2018.0108.

Charak, R., Vang, M. L., Shevlin, M., et al. (2020). Lifetime interpersonal victimization profiles and mental health problems in a nationally representative panel of trauma-exposed adults in the United Kingdom. *Journal of Traumatic Stress, 33,* 654–664. https://doi.org/10.1002/jts.22527.

Charteris-Black, J. (2006). Britain as a container: Immigration metaphors in the 2005 campaign. *Discourse & Society, 17*, 563–581. https://doi.org/10.1177/0957926506066345.

Chauhan, A., & Foster, J. (2013). Representations of poverty in British newspapers: A case of "othering" the threat. *Journal of Community and Applied Social Psychology, 24*, 390–405. https://doi.org/10.1002/casp.2179.

Chekol, M. A., Moges, M. A., & Nigatu, B. A. (2023). Social media hate speech in the walk of Ethiopian political reform: Analysis of hate speech prevalence, severity, and natures. *Information, Communication & Society, 26*, 218–237. https://doi.org/10.1080/1369118x.2021.1942955.

Chhabra, A., & Vishwakarma, D. K. (2023). A literature survey on multimodal and multilingual automatic speech identification. *Multimedia Systems, 29*, 1203–1230. https://doi.org/10.1007/s00530-023-01051-8.

Chong, D. (2006). Free speech and multiculturalism in and out of the academy. *Political Psychology, 27*, 29–54. https://doi.org/10.1111/J.1467-9221.2006.00448.x.

Christodoulides, G., Gerrath, M. H. E. E., & Siamagka, N. T. (2021). Don't be rude! The effect of content moderation on consumer-brand forgiveness. *Psychology & Marketing, 38*, 1686–1699. https://doi.org/10.1002/mar.21458.

Chu, C., & Ashburn-Nardo, L. (2022). Black Americans' perspectives on ally confrontations of racial prejudice. *Journal of Experimental Social Psychology, 101*, 1–9. https://doi.org/10.1016/j.jesp.2022.104337.

Cialdini, R. B., Reno, R. R., & Kallgren, C. A. (1990). A focus theory of normative conduct: Recycling the concept of norms to reduce littering in public places. *Journal of Personality and Social Psychology, 58*, 1015–1026. https://doi.org/10.1037/0022-3514.58.6.1015.

Cohen-Almagor, R. (2008). Hate in the classroom: Free expression, Holocaust denial, and liberal education. *American Journal of Education, 114*, 215–241. https://doi.org/10.1086/524316.

Comas-Díaz, L., Hall, G. N., & Neville, H. A. (2019). Racial trauma: Theory, research, and healing: Introduction to the special issue. *American Psychologist, 74*, 1–5. https://doi.org/10.1037/amp0000442.

Cornell Law School. United States Constitution Annotated. www.law.cornell.edu/constitution-conan.

Cortina, L. M., Kabat-Farr, D., Leskinen, E. A., Huerta, M., & Magley, V. J. (2011). Selective incivility as modern discrimination in organizations: Evidence and impact. *Journal of Management, 39*, 1579–1605. https://doi.org/10.1177/0149206311418835.

Costello, M., Hawdon, J., & Ratliff, T. N. (2017). Confronting online extremism: The effect of self-help, collective efficacy, and guardianship on being a target for hate speech. *Social Science Computer Review, 35,* 587–605. https://doi.org/10.1177/0894439316666272.

Costello, K., & Hodson, G. (2009). Exploring the roots of dehumanization: The role of animal-human similarity in promoting immigrant humanization. *Group Processes & Intergroup Relations, 13,* 3–22. https://doi.org/10.1177/1368430209347725.

Cottrell, C. A., & Neuberg, S. L. (2005). Different emotional reactions to different groups: A sociofunctional threat-based approach to "prejudice". *Journal of Personality and Social Psychology, 88,* 770–789. https://doi.org/10.1037/0022-3514.88.5.770.

Council of Europe Committee of Ministers (1997). Recommendation No. R (97) 20 of the Committee of Ministers to Member States on "Hate Speech." https://rm.coe.int/1680505d5b.

Cowan, G., Heiple, B., Marquez, C., Khatchadourian, D., & McNevin, M. (2005). Heterosexuals' attitudes toward hate crimes and hate speech against gays and lesbians: Old-fashioned and modern heterosexism. *Journal of Homosexuality, 49,* 67–82. https://doi.org/10.1300/J082V49N02_04.

Cowan, G., & Hodge, C. (1996). Judgments of hate speech: The effects of target group, publicness, and behavioral responses of the target. *Journal of Applied Psychology, 26,* 4. 9–62. https://doi.org/10.1111/j.1559-1816.1996.tb01854.x.

Cowan, G., & Mettrick, J. (2002). The effect of target variables and setting on perceptions of hate speech. *Journal of Applied Social Psychology, 32,* 277–299. https://doi.org/10.1111/J.1559-1816.2002.TB00213.x.

Cowan, G., Resendez, M., Marshall, E., & Quist, R. (2002). Hate speech and constitutional protection: Priming values of equality and freedom. *Journal of Social Issues, 58,* 247–263. https://doi.org/10.1111/1540-4560.00259.

Cralley, E. L., & Ruscher, J. B. (2005). Lady, girl, female, or woman: Sexism and cognitive busyness predict use of gender-biased nouns. *Journal of Language and Social Psychology, 24,* 300–314. https://doi.org/10.1177/0261927X05278391.

Crandall, C. S., Eshleman, A., & O'Brien, L. (2002). Social norms and the expression and suppression of prejudice: The struggle for internalization. *Journal of Personality and Social Psychology, 82,* 359–378. https://doi.org/10.1037/0022-3514.82.3.359.

Crown Prosecution Service (2023, November). CPS North East-Successful Hate Crime Prosecutions. www.cps.gov.uk/north-east/news/cps-north-east-successful-hate-crime-prosecutions-november-2023.

Culpeper, J. (2021). Impoliteness and hate speech: Compare and contrast. *Journal of Pragmatics*, *179*, 4–11. https://doi.org/10.1016/j.pragma.2021.04.019.

Curran, G. (2004). Mainstreaming populist discourse: The race-conscious legacy of neo-populist parties in Australia and Italy. *Patterns of Prejudice*, *38*, 37–55. https://doi.org/10.1080/0031322032000185578.

Czopp, A. M., Monteith, M. J., & Mark, A. Y. (2006). Standing up for a change: Reducing bias through interpersonal confrontation. *Journal of Personality and Social Psychology*, *90*, 784–803. https://doi.org/10.1037/0022-3514.90.5.784.

Dai, J. D., Lopez, J. J., Brady, L. M., Eason, A. E., & Fryberg, S. A. (2021). Erasing and dehumanizing Natives to protect positive national identity: The Native mascot example. *Social and Personality Psychology Compass*, *15*, e12632. https://doi.org/10.1111/SPC3.12632.

Danso, H. A., Sedlovskaya, A., & Suanda, S. H. (2007). Perceptions of immigrants: Modifying the attitudes of individuals higher in social dominance orientation. *Personality and Social Psychology Bulletin*, *33*, 1113–1123. https://doi.org/10.1177/0146167207301015.

Daumiller, M., & Janke, S. (2020). Effects of performance goals and social norms on academic dishonesty in a test. *British Journal of Educational Psychology*, *90*, 537–559. https://doi.org/10.1111/bjep.12310.

Delgado, R., & Stefancic, J. (2023). *Critical race theory* 4th ed. New York: New York University Press.

Desai, D. (2010). The challenge of new colorblind racism in art education. *Art Education*, *63*, 22–28. https://doi.org/10.1080/00043125.2010.11519084.

Devine, P. G., Monteith, M. J., Zuwerink, J. R., & Elliot, A. J. (1991). Prejudice with and without compunction. *Journal of Personality and Social Psychology*, *60*, 817–830. https://doi.org/10.1037/0022-3514.60.6.817.

Douglas, K. M., & Sutton, R. M. (2014). "A giant leap for mankind" but what about women? The role of system-justifying ideologies in predicting attitudes toward sexist language. *Journal of Language and Social Psychology*, *33*, 667–680. https://doi.org/10.1177/0261927X14538638.

Døving, C. A., & Emberland, T. (2021). Bringing the enemy closer to home: "Conspiracy talk" and the Norwegian far right. *Patterns of Prejudice*, *55*, 375–390. https://doi.org/10.1080/0031322X.2021.1909933.

Duchscherer, K. M., & Dovidio, J. F. (2016). When memes are mean: Appraisals of and objections to stereotypic memes. *Translational Issues in Psychological Science*, *2*, 335–345. https://doi.org/10.1037/tps0000080.

Dunlap, J., Chamberlain, A. W., Wesaw, A., & Parnell, A. (2023). Advancing Racial Justice on Campus. National Association of Student Personnel

Administrators (NASPA). www.naspa.org/report/advancing-racial-justice-on-campus-student-and-administrator-perspectives-on-conditions-for-change.

Ellingworth, D., Bécares, L., Štastná, M., & Nazroo, J. (2023). 4: Racism and racial discrimination. In N. Finney, J. Nazroo, L. Bécares, D. Kapadia, & N. Shlomo (Eds.), *Racism and Ethnic Inequality in a Time of Crisis* (pp. 54–77). Bristol: Policy Press. https://doi.org/10.51952/9781447368861.ch004.

Ellis, N. T. (August, 2023). Florida's New Standards on Black History Curriculum Are Creating Outrage www.cnn.com/2023/08/17/us/florida-black-history-backlash-reaj/index.html.

El Refaie, E. (2001). Metaphors we discriminate by: Naturalized themes in Austrian newspaper articles about asylum seekers. *Journal of Sociolinguistics*, *5*, 352–371. https://doi.org/10.1111/1467-9481.00154.

Esses, V. M., Medianu, S., & Lawson, A. S. (2013). Uncertainty, threat, and the role of the media in promoting the dehumanization of immigrants and refugees. *Journal of Social Issues*, *69*, 518–536. https://doi.org/10.1111/josi.12027.

Fasoli, F., Maass, A., & Carnaghi, A. (2015). Labelling and discrimination: Do homophobic epithets undermine fair distribution of resources. *British Journal of Social Psychology*, *54*, 383–393. https://doi.org/10.1111/bjso.12090.

Fasoli, F., Paladino, M. P., Carnaghi, A., et al. (2016). Not "just words": Exposure to homophobic epithets leads to dehumanizing and physical distancing from gay men. *European Journal of Social Psychology*, *46*, 237–248. https://doi.org/10.0002/ejsp.2148.

Fiske, S. T. (1998). Stereotyping, prejudice, and discrimination. In D. T. Gilbert, S. T. Fiske, & G. Lindzey (Eds.), *Handbook of social psychology*, Vol. 2. 4th ed. (pp. 357–411). New York: McGraw-Hill.

Fiske, S. T. (2018). Stereotype content: Warmth and competence endure. *Current Directions in Psychological Science*, *27*, 67–73. https://doi.org/10.1177/0963721417738825.

Flanders, C. E. (2015). Bisexual health: A daily diary analysis of stress and anxiety. *Basic and Applied Social Psychology*, *37*, 319–335. https://doi.org/10.1080/01973533.2015.1079202.

Forscher, P. S., Cox, W. T. L., Graetz, N., & Devine, P. G. (2015). The motivation to express prejudice. *Journal of Personality and Social Psychology*, *109*, 791–812. https://doi.org/10.1037/pspi0000030.

Frankish, T., & Bradbury, J. (2012). Telling stories for the next generation: Trauma and nostalgia. *Peace and Conflict: Journal of Peace Psychology*, *8*, 294–306. https://doi.org/10.1037/a0029070.

Fryberg, S. A., & Eason, A. E. (2017). Making the invisible visible: Acts of commission and omission. *Current Directions in Psychological Science, 26,* 554–559. https://doi.org/10.1177/0963721417720959.

Galbiati, R., Henry, E., Jacquemet, N., & Lobeck, M. (2021). How laws affect the perception of norms: Empirical evidence from the lockdown. *PLoS One, 16,* e0256624. https://doi.org/10.1371/journal.pone.0256624.

Gallagher, C. (2022, October 13). Text Messages between Oath Keepers Founder and Lawyer Not Protected, U.S. Judge Rules. www.reuters.com/legal/text-messages-between-oath-keepers-founder-lawyer-not-protected-us-judge-rules-2022-10-13/.

Gelber, K., & McNamara, L. (2015). The effects of civil hate speech laws: Lessons from Australia. *Law & Society Review, 49,* 631–664. https://doi.org/10.1111/lasr.12152.

Gelber, K., & McNamara, L. (2016). Evidencing the harms of hate speech. *Social Identities, 22,* 324–341. https://doi.org/10.1080/13504630.2015.1128810.

Gerstenfeld, P. B., Grant, D. R., & Chiang, C.-P. (2003). Hate online: A content analysis of extremist internet sites. *Analyses of Social Issues and Public Policy, 3,* 29–44. https://doi.org/10.1111/J.1530-2415.2003.00013.x.

Glasman, L. R., & Albarricín, D. (2006). Forming attitudes that predict future behavior: A meta-analysis of the attitude-behavior relation. *Psychological Bulletin, 132,* 778–822. https://doi.org/10.1037/0033-2909.132.5.778.

Glick, P., Fiske, S. T., Mladinic, A., et al. (2000). Beyond prejudice as simple antipathy: Hostile and benevolent sexism across cultures. *Journal of Personality and Social Psychology, 79,* 763–775. https://doi.org/10.1037/0022-3514.79.5.763.

Goff, P., Eberhardt, J., Williams, M., & Jackson, M. (2008). Not yet human: Implicit knowledge, historical dehumanization, and contemporary consequences. *Journal of Personality and Social Psychology, 94,* 292–306. https://doi.org/10.1037/0022-3514.94.2.292.

Goff, P. A., Jackson, M. C., Di Leone, B. A. L., Culotta, C. M., & DiTomasso, N. A. (2014). The essence of innocence: Consequences of dehumanizing Black children. *Journal of Personality and Social Psychology, 106,* 526–545. https://doi.org/10.1037/a0035663.

Goldman-Hasbun, J. (2023). The moral discourse of free speech: A virtual ethnographic study. *Journal of Contemporary Ethnography, 2,* 463–492. https://doi.org/10.1177/08912416221129880.

Good, J. J., Moss-Racusin, C. A., & Sanchez, D. T. (2012). When do we confront? Perceptions of costs and benefits predict confronting discrimination on behalf of self and others. *Psychology of Women Quarterly, 36,* 210–226. https://doi.org/10.1177/0361684312440958.

Goodman, J. A., Schell, J., Alexander, M. G., & Eidelman, S. (2008). The impact of a derogatory remark on prejudice toward a gay male leader. *Journal of Applied Social Psychology, 38,* 542–555. https://doi.org/10.1111/j.1559-1816.2008.00316.x.

Grabowski, M., Dinh, T. K., Wu, W., & Stockdale, M. S. (2022). The sex-based harassment inventory: A gender status threat measure of sex-based harassment intentions. *Sex Roles, 86,* 648–666. https://doi.org/10.007/s11199-022-01294-1.

Gray, K. L., & Stein, K. (2021). "We 'said her name' and got zucked:" Black women calling-out the carceral logics of digital platforms. *Gender & Society, 35,* 538–545. https://doi.org/10.1177/08912432211029393.

Greenberg, J., & Pyszczynski, T. (1985). The effects of an overheard ethnic slur on evaluations of the target: How to spread a social disease. *Journal of Experimental Social Psychology, 21,* 61–72. https://doi.org/10.1016/0022-1031(85)90006-X.

Grupe, D. W., & Nitschke, J. B. (2013). Uncertainty and anticipation in anxiety: An integrated neurobiological and psychological perspective. *Nature Reviews Neuroscience, 14,* 488–501. https://doi.org/10.1038/nrn3524.

Guglielmo, T. A. (2004). *White on arrival: Italians, race, color, and power in Chicago, 1890–1945.* New York: Oxford University Press.

Gulker, J. E., Mark, A. Y., & Montcith, M. J. (2013). Confronting prejudice: The who, what, and why of confrontation effectiveness. *Social Influence, 8,* 280–293. https://doi.org/10.1080/15534510.2012.736879.

Gutierrez, L. J., & Unzueta, M. M. (2021). My kind of guy: Social dominance orientation, hierarchy-relevance, and tolerance of racist job candidates. *Personality and Social Psychology Bulletin, 48,* 659–675. https://doi.org/10.1177/01461672211011031.

Guynn, J. (2020). Facebook while black: Users call it getting "zucked," say talking about racism is censored as hate speech. *USA Today,* 9 July. www.usatoday.com/story/news/2019/04/24/facebook-while-black-zuckedusers-say-they-get-blocked-racism-discussion/2859593002/.

Hangartner, D., Gennaro, G., Alasiri, S., et al. (2021). Empathy-based counter-speech can reduce racist hate speech in a social media field experiment. *PNAS Proceedings of the National Academy of Sciences, 118,* e2116310118.

Hansen, K., & Dovidio, J. F. (2016). Social dominance orientation, nonnative accents, and hiring recommendations. *Cultural Diversity and Ethnic Minority Psychology, 22,* 544–551. https://doi.org/10.1037/cdp0000101.

Harlow, S., & Benbrook, A. (2019). How #Blacklivesmatter: Exploring the role of hip-hop celebrities in constructing racial identity on Black Twitter,

Information. *Communication & Society*, *22*, 352–368. https://doi.org/10.1080/1369118X.2017.1386705.

Harris, L. T., & Fiske, S. T. (2006). Social neuroscience evidence for dehumanized perception. *European Review of Social Psychology*, *20*, 192–231. https://doi.org/10.1080/10463280902954988.

Harwood, S. A., Huntt, M. B., Mendenhall, R., & Lewis, J. A. (2012). Racial microaggressions in the residence halls: Experiences of students of color at a predominantly White university. *Journal of Diversity in Higher Education*, *5*, 159–173. https://doi.org/10.1037/a0028956.

Haslam, N., Bain, P., Douge, L., Lee, M., & Bastian, B. (2005). More human than you: Attributing humanness to self and others. *Journal of Personality and Social Psychology*, *89*, 937–950. https://doi.org/10.1037/0022-3514.89.6.937.

Hermida, P. C. de Q., & Santos, E. M. d. (2023). Detecting hate speech in memes: A review. *Artificial Intelligence Review*, *56*, 12833–12851. https://doi.org/10.1007/S10462-023-10459-7.

Heumann, M., & Church, T. W. (1997). *Hate speech on campus: Cases, case studies, and commentary*. Boston, MA: Northeastern University Press.

Hietanen, M., & Eddebo, J. (2023). Towards a definition of hate speech – with a focus on online contexts. *Journal of Communication Inquiry*, *47*, 343–500. https://doi.org/10.1177/01968599221124309.

Hildebrand, L. K., Jusuf, C. C., & Monteith, M. J. (2020). Ally confrontations as identity-safety cues for marginalized individuals. *European Journal of Social Psychology*, *50*, 1318–1333. https://doi.org/10.1002/ejsp.2692.

Hodson, G., Rush, J., & Macinnis, C. C. (2010). A joke is just a joke (except when it isn't): Cavalier humor beliefs facilitate the expression of group dominance motives. *Journal of Personality and Social Psychology*, *99*, 660–682. https://doi.org/10.1037/a0019627.

Hopton, K., & Langer, S. (2021). "Kick the XX out of your life": An analysis of the manosphere's discursive constructions of gender on Twitter. *Feminism & Psychology*, *32*, 3–22. https://doi.org/10.1177/09593535211033461.

Houston, D., M., & Andreopoulou, A. (2003). Tests of both corollaries of social identity theory's self-esteem hypothesis in real group settings. *British Journal of Social Psychology*, *42*, 357–370. https://doi.org/10.1348/014466603322438206.

Hsieh, W., Faulkner, N., & Wickes, R. (2022). What reduces prejudice in the real world? A meta-analysis of prejudice reduction field experiments. *British Journal of Social Psychology*, *61*, 689–710. https://doi.org/10.1111/bjso.12509.

Hsueh, M., Yogeeswaran, K., & Malinen, S. (2015). "Leave your comment below": Can biased online comments influence our own prejudicial attitudes and behaviors? *Human Communication Research, 41*, 557–576. https://doi.org/10.1111/hcre.12059.

Huang, J. T., Krupenkin, M., Rothschild, D., & Cunningham, J. L. (2022). The cost of anti-Asian racism during the COVID-19 pandemic. *Nature Human Behaviour, 7*, 682–695. https://doi.org/10.1038/s41562-022-01493-6.

Hurd, N. M., Trawalter, S., Jakubow, A., Johnson, H. E., & Billingsley, J. T. (2022). Online racial discrimination and the role of White bystanders. *American Psychologist, 77*, 39–55. https://doi.org/10.1037/amp0000603.

Huynh, V. W., Raval, V. V., & Freeman, M. (2022). Ethnic-racial discrimination toward Asian Americans amidst COVID-19, the so-called "China" virus and associations with mental health. *Asian American Journal of Psychology, 13*, 259–269. https://doi.org/10.1037/aap0000264.

Inara Rodis, P. d. C. (2021). Let's (re)tweet about racism and sexism: Responses to cyber aggression toward Black and Asian women. *Information, Communication & Society, 24*, 2153–2173. https://doi.org/10.1080/136118x.2021.1962948.

International Convention on the Elimination of All Forms of Racial Discrimination. (1969). www.ohchr.org/en/instruments-mechanisms/instruments/international-convention-elimination-all-forms-racial.

Jacob, G., Faber, S. C., Faber, N., et al. (2023). A systematic review of Black people coping with racism: Approaches, analysis, and empowerment. *Perspectives on Psychological Science, 18*, 392–415. https://doi.org/10.1177/17456916221100509.

Jacobs, L., & van Spanje, J. (2021). Martyrs for free speech? Disentangling the effects of legal prosecution of anti-immigration politicians on their electoral support. *Political Behavior, 43*, 973–996. https://doi.org/10/1007/s11109-019-09581-6.

Jimenez, T., Arndt, J., & Landau, M. J. (2021). Walls block waves: Using an inundation metaphor of immigration predicts support for a border wall. *Journal of Social and Political Psychology, 9*, 159–171. https://doi.org/10.5964/jspp.6383.

Johnson, V. E., Nadal, K. L., Sissoko, D. R. G., & King, R. (2021). "It's not in your head": Gaslighting, splaining, victim blaming, and other harmful reactions to microaggressions. *Perspectives on Psychological Science, 16*, 1024–1036. https://doi.org/10.1177/17456916211011963.

Joseph, R. L. (2011). Imagining Obama: Reading overtly and inferentially racist images of our 44th President, 2007–2008. *Communication Studies, 62*, 389–405. https://doi.org/10.1080/10510974.2011.588074.

Jung, C. W. (2023). Role of informal social control in predicting racist hate speech on online platforms: Collective efficacy and the theory of planned behavior. *Cyberpsychology, Behavior, and Social Networking, 26,* 507–518. https://doi.org/10.1089/cyber.2022.0107.

Kafka, A. (2023). Seeing through woke-washing: Effects of projected diversity values and leader racial diversity on equity in workplace outcomes. *Consulting Psychology Journal, 75,* 94–119. https://doi.org/10.1037/cpb0000237.

Kamenetz, A., Lattimore, K., & Depenbrock, J. (2017, June). Harvard Rescinds Admission of 10 Students over Obscene Facebook Messages. www.npr.org/sections/ed/2017/06/06/531591202/harvard-rescinds-admission-of-10-students-over-obscene-facebook-messages.

Kansok-Dusche, J., Ballaschk, C., Krause, N., et al. (2022). A systematic review on hate speech among children and adolescents: Definitions, prevalence, and overlap with related phenomena. *Trauma, Violence, & Abuse, 24,* 2598–615. https://doi.org/10.1177/15248380221108070.

Kendall, M. (November 16, 2016). 22 Times Michelle Obama Endured Rude, Racist, Sexist or Plain Ridiculous Attacks. www.washingtonpost.com/posteverything/wp/2016/11/16/22-times-michelle-obama-endured-rude-racist-sexist-or-plain-dumb-attacks/.

Kesebir, P., & Pyszczynski, T. (2011). A moral-existential account of psychological factors fostering intergroup conflict. *Personality and Social Psychology Compass, 5,* 878–890. https://doi.org/10.1111/j.1751-9004.2011.00397.x.

Keum, B. T., & Hearns, M. (2022). Online gaming and racism: Impact on psychological distress among Black, Asian, and Latinx emerging adults. *Games and Culture, 17,* 445–460. https://doi.org/10.1177/15554120211039082.

King, E. B., Hebl, M., Shapiro, J. R., et al. (2024). (Absent) allyship in STEM: Can psychological standing increase prejudice confrontation. *Journal of Business and Psychology.* https://doi.org/10.1007/S10869-023-09929-0.

Kirkland, S. L., Greenberg, J., & Pyszczynski, T. (1987). Further evidence of the deleterious effects of overheard derogatory ethnic labels: Derogation beyond the target. *Personality and Social Psychology Bulletin, 13,* 216–227. https://doi.org/10.1077/0146167287132007.

Klein, A. (2010). *A space for hate: The White power movement's adaptation into cyberspace.* Duluth, MN: Litwin.

Kneale, D., & Bécares, L. (2023). The influence of a hostile environment on a syndemic of depression, stress and chronic limiting illness among LGBTQ+ people during the COVID-19 pandemic. *Sociology of Health & Illness, 46,* 114–136. https://doi.org/10.1111/1467-9566.13689.

Krahé, B., Möller, I., Huesmann, L. R., et al. (2011). Desensitization to media violence: Links with habitual media violence exposure, aggressive cognitions, and aggressive behavior. *Journal of Personality and Social Psychology, 100*, 630–646. https://doi.org/10.1037/a0021711.

Lakoff, G., & Johnson, M. (1980). *Metaphors we live by.* Chicago, IL: University of Chicago Press.

Lamb, L. M., Bigler, R. S., Liben, L. S., & Green, V. A. (2009). Teaching children to confront peers' sexist remarks: Implications for theories of gender development and educational practice. *Sex Roles, 61*, 361–382. https://doi.org/10.1007/s11199-009-9634-4.

Lamont, M., Park, B. Y., & Ayala-Hurtado, E. (2017). Trump's electoral speeches and his appeal to the American white working class. *British Journal of Sociology, 68*, 153–180. https://doi.org/10.1111/1468-4446.12315.

Landau, M. J., Meier, B. P., & Keefer, L. A. (2010). A metaphor-enriched social cognition. *Psychological Bulletin, 136*, 1045–1067. https://doi.org/10.1037/a0020970.

Lee, I.-C., Pratto, F., & Johnson, B. T. (2011). Intergroup consensus/disagreement in support of group-based hierarchy: An examination of socio-structural and psycho-cultural factors. *Psychological Bulletin, 137*, 1029–1064. https://doi.org/10.1037/a0025410.

Leets, L. (2002). Experiencing hate speech: Perceptions and responses to anti-Semitism and antigay speech. *Journal of Social Issues, 58*, 341–361. https://doi.org/10.1111/1540-4560.00264.

Lee-Won, R. J., White, T. N., Song, H., Lee, J. Y., & Smith, M. R. (2020). Source magnification of cyberhate: Affective and cognitive effects of multiple-source hate messages on target members. *Media Psychology, 23*, 603–624. https://doi.org/10.1080/15213269.2019.16112760.

Leskinen, E. A., Rabelo, B. C., & Cortina, L. M. (2015). Gender stereotyping and harassment: A "Catch-22" for women in the workplace. *Psychology, Public Policy, and Law, 21*, 192–204. https://doi.org/10.1037/law0000040.

Levin, A. (2010). *The cost of free speech: Pornography, hate speech, and their challenge to liberalism.* England: Palgrave Macmillan.

Linz, D. G., Donnerstein, E., & Penrod, S. (1988). Effects of long-term exposure to violent and sexually degrading depictions of women. *Journal of Personality and Social Psychology, 55*, 758–768. https://doi.org/10.1037/0022-3514.55.5.758.

Lott, T. L. (1999). *The invention of race: Black culture and the politics of representation.* Malden, MA: Blackwell.

Loughnan, S., Haslam, N., Sutton, R. M., & Spencer, B. (2014). Dehumanization and social class: Animality in the stereotypes of "white trash," "chavs," and "bogans." *Social Psychology, 45*, 54–61. https://doi.org/10.1027/1864-9335/A000159.

Maass, A., Salvi, D., Arcuri, L., & Semin, G. (1989). Language use in intergroup contexts: The linguistic intergroup bias. *Journal of Personality and Social Psychology, 57*, 981–993. https://doi.org/10.1037/0022-3514.57.6.981.

MacAvaney, S., Yao, H.-R., Yang, E., et al. (2019). Hate speech detection: Challenges and solutions. *PLoS ONE, 14*, e0221152. https://doi.org/10.1371/journal.pone.0221152.

Malcolm, F. (2021). Silencing and freedom of speech in UK higher education. *British Educational Research Journal, 47*, 52–538. https://doi.org/10.1002/berj.3661.

Martínez, C., van Prooijen, J.-W., & Van Lange, P. A. M. (2022). A threat-based hate model: How symbolic and realistic threats underlie hate and aggression. *Journal of Experimental Social Psychology, 103*, 1–13. https://doi.org/10.1016/JESP.2022.104393.

Martinez, L. R., Hebl, M. R., Smith, N. A., & Sabat, I. E. (2017). Standing up and speaking out against prejudice toward gay men in the workplace. *Journal of Vocational Behavior, 103*, 71–85. https://doi.org/10.1016/j.jvb.2017.08.001.

Mathew, B., Illendula, A., Saha, P., et al. (2020). Hate begets hate: A temporal study of hate speech. *Proceedings of Association for Computing Machinery, 4*, 92. 1–24. https://doi.org/10.1145/3415163.

Matsuda, M. J., Lawrence, C. R., Delgado, R., & Crenshaw, K. W. (1993). *Words that wound*. Boulder, CO: Westview Press.

Matsumoto, D., Frank, M. G., & Hwang, H. C. (2015). The role of intergroup emotions in political violence. *Current Directions in Psychological Science, 24*, 369–373. https://doi.org/10.1177/0963721415595023.

Matsumoto, D., Hwang, H. C., & Frank, M. G. (2016). The effects of incidental anger, contempt, and disgust on hostile language and implicit behaviors. *Journal of Applied Social Psychology, 46*, 437–452. https://doi.org/10.1111/jasp.12374.

Matsumoto, D., Hwang, H. C., & Frank, M. G. (2017). Emotion and aggressive intergroup cognitions: The ANCODI hypothesis. *Aggressive Behavior, 43*, 93–107. https://doi.org/10.1002/ab.21666.

McGee, T., & Kruger, A. C. (2022). Racial microaggressions and African American undergraduates' academic experiences: Preparation for bias messages as a protective resource. *Journal of Black Psychology, 48,* 726–775. https://doi.org/10.1177/00957984211067628.

McNamee, L. G., Peterson, B. L., & Peña, J. (2010). A call to education, participate, invoke, and indict: Understanding the communication of online hate groups. *Communication Monographs, 77,* 257–280. https://doi.org/10.1080/03637751003758227.

Mekawi, Y., & Todd, N. R. (2018). Okay to say?: Initial validation of the acceptability of racial microaggressions scale. *Cultural Diversity and Ethnic Minority Psychology, 24,* 346–362. https://doi.org/10.1037/CDP0000201.

Mendelsohn, J., Tsvetkov, Y., & Jurafsky, D. (2020). A framework for the computational linguistic analysis of dehumanization. *Frontiers in Artificial Intelligence, 3,* 1–24. https://doi.org/10.3389/frai.2020.00055.

Merritt, S. K., O'Brien, L. T., & Ruscher, J. B. (2021). Creating clever internet memes perpetuates offensiveness. *Western Journal of Communication, 85,* 471–486. https://doi.org/10.1080/10570314.2020.1800812.

Moran, L. (2018). Fox News Host Tucker Carlson Says Immigration Is Making America "Dirtier." www.huffpost.com/entry/tucker-carlson-immigrants-doing-to-america_n_5c136ca1e4b0f60cfa27dbaf.

Moses, M. S. (2021). "Very fine people on both sides": Diverse viewpoints, truth, and free speech on campus. *Educational Studies, 57,* 365–377. https://doi.org/10.1080/00131946.2021.1945608.

Mozafari, M., Farahbakhsh, R., & Crespi, N. (2020). Hate speech detection and racial bias mitigation in social media based on BERT model. *PLoS ONE, 15,* e0237861. https://doi.org/10.1371/journal.pone.0237861.

Mullen, B., & Johnson, C. (1993). Cognitive representation in ethnophaulisms as a function of group size: The phenomenology of being in a group. *Personality and Social Psychology Bulletin, 19,* 296–304. https://doi.org/10.1177/0146167293193006.

Mullen, B., & Smyth, J. M. (2004). Immigrant suicide rates as a function of ethnophaulisms: Hate speech predicts death. *Psychosomatic Medicine, 66,* 343–348. https://doi.org/10.1097/01.psy.0000126197.59447.b3.

Mulvey, K. L., Palmer, S. B., & Abrams, D. (2016). Race-based humor and peer group dynamics in adolescence: Bystander intervention and social exclusion. *Child Development, 87,* 1379–1391. https://doi.org/10.1111/cdev.12600.

Murphy, M. C., Richeson, J. A., Shelton, J. N., Rheinschmidt, M. L., & Bergsieker, H. B. (2012). Cognitive costs of contemporary prejudice. *Group Processes and Intergroup Relations, 16,* 560–571. https://doi.org/10.1177/1368430212468170.

Musolff, A. (2007). What role do metaphors play in racial prejudice? The function of antisemitic imagery in Hitler's *Mein Kamp*. *Patterns of Prejudice, 1*, 21–43. https://doi.org/10.1080/00313220601118744.

Nature Human Behaviour Editorial (2018). The cooperative human. *Nature Human Behaviour, 2*, 427–428. https://doi.org/10.1038/s41562-018-0389.

Nelson, J. C., Adams, G., & Salter, P. S. (2012). The Marley hypothesis: Denial of racism reflects ignorance of history. *Psychological Science, 24*, 213–218. https://doi.org/10.1177/0956797612451466.

Nelson, J. K., Dunn, K. M., & Paradies, Y. (2011). Bystander anti-racism: A review of the literature. *Analyses of Social Issues and Public Policy, 11*, 263–284. https://doi.org/10.1111/j.1530-2415.2011.01274.x.

Nielsen, L. B. (2002). Subtle, pervasive, harmful: Racist and sexist remarks in public as hate speech. *Journal of Social Issues, 58*, 265–280. https://doi.org/10.1111/1540-4560.00260.

Nisbett, R. E., Krantz, D. H., Jepson, C., & Kunda, Z. (1983). The use of statistical heuristics in everyday inductive reasoning. *Psychological Review, 90*, 339–363. https://doi.org/10.1037/0033-295X.90.4.339.

Noor, M., Shnabel, N., Halabi, S., & Nadler, A. (2012). When suffering begets suffering: The psychology of competitive victimhood between adversarial groups in violent conflicts. *Personality and Social Psychology Review, 16*, 351–374. https://doi.org/10.1177/1088868312440048.

Nugent, W. R., Abrams, T. E., & Joseph, A. A. (2022). The relationship between political rhetoric and mass shootings. *Journal of Social Service Research, 48*, 246–258. https://doi.org/10.1080/01488376.2021.2018089.

O'Brien, L. T., Blodorn, A., Alsbrooks, A., et al. (2009). Understanding White Americans' perceptions of racism in Hurricane Katrina-related events. *Group Processes and Intergroup Relations, 12*, 431–444. https://doi.org/10.1177/1368430209105047.

O'Brien, L. T., & Merritt, S. (2022). Attributions to discrimination against Black victims in a multiracial society: Isolating the effect of perpetrator group membership. *Personality and Social Psychology Bulletin, 48*, 120–134. https://doi.org/10.1177/0146167220988372.

Oliva, T. D., Antonialli, D. M., & Gomes, A. (2021). Fighting hate speech, silencing drag queens? Artificial intelligence in content moderation and risks to LGBTQ voice online. *Sexuality & Culture, 25*, 700–732. https://doi.org/10.1007/S12119-020-09790-w.

O'Neal, E. C., & Taylor, S. L. (1989). Status of the provoker, opportunity to retaliate, and interest in video violence. *Aggressive Behavior, 15*, 171–180. https://doi.org/10.1002/1098-2337(1989)15:2.

Ong, A. D., Cerrada, C., Lee, R. A., & Williams, D. R. (2017). Stigma consciousness, racial microaggressions, and sleep disturbance among Asian Americans. *Asian American Journal of Psychology, 8,* 72–81. https://doi.org/10.1037/aap0000062.

Onyeador, I. N., Hudson, S. T. J., & Lewis, N. A. (2021). Moving beyond implicit bias training: Policy insights for increasing organizational diversity. *Policy Insights from the Behavioral and Brain Sciences, 8,* 19–26. https://doi.org/10.117/2372732220983840.

Orehek, E., & Weaverling, C. G. (2017). On the nature of objectification: Implications of considering people as means to goals. *Perspectives on Psychological Science, 12,* 703–921. https://doi.org/10.1177/1745691617691138.

Ortiz, S. M. (2019). "You can say I got desensitized to it": How men of color cope with everyday racism in online gaming. *Sociological Perspectives, 62,* 572–588. https://doi.org/10.1177/0731121419837588.

Pabian, S., Vandebosch, H., Poels, K., Van Cleemput, K., & Bastiaensens, S. (2016). Exposure to cyberbullying as a bystander: An investigation of desensitization effects among early adolescents. *Computers in Human Behavior, 62,* 480–487. https://doi.org/10.1016/J.chb.2016.04.022.

Panaitiu, I. G. (2020). Apes and anticitizens: Simianization and U.S. national identity discourse. *Social Identities, 26,* 109–127. https://doi.org/10.1080/13504630.2019.1679621.

Parker, L. R., Monteith, M. J., Moss-Racusin, C. A., & Van Camp, A. R. (2018). Promoting concern about gender bias with evidence-based confrontation. *Journal of Experimental Social Psychology, 74,* 8–23. https://doi.org/10.1016/j.jesp.2017.07.009.

Paterson, J. L., Brown, R., & Walters, M. (2019). The short and longer term impacts of hate crimes experienced directly, indirectly, and through the media. *Personality and Social Psychology Bulletin, 45,* 994–1010. https://doi.org/10.1177/0146167218802835.

Payne, B. K., & Correll, J. (2020). Race, weapons, and the perception of threat. *Advances in Experimental Social Psychology, 62,* 1–50. https://doi.org/10.1016/bs.aesp.2020.04.001.

Peirce, K., & McBride, M. (1999). Aunt Jemima isn't keeping up with the energizer bunny: Stereotyping of animated spokescharacters in advertising. *Sex Roles, 40,* 959–968. https://doi.org/1023/A.1018833423803.

Pettersson, K. (2019). "Freedom of speech requires actions": Exploring the discourse of politicians convicted of hate-speech against Muslims. *European Journal of Social Psychology, 49,* 938–952. https://doi.org/10.1002/ejsp.2577.

Pew Research Center (2013). A Survey of LGBT Americans. www.pewsocial trends.org/2013/06/13/a-survey-of-lgbt-americans/.

Pew Research Center (2016). Americans More Tolerant of Offensive Speech than Others in the World. www.pewresearch.org/fact-tank/2016/10/12/ameri cans-more-tolerant-of-offensive-speech-than-others-in-the-world/.

Pew Research Center (2022). Alternative Social Media Sites Frequently Identify as Free Speech Advocates. www.pewresearch.org/journalism/ 2022/10/06/alternative-social-media-sites-frequently-identify-as-free-speech-advocates/.

Pew Research Center (2024). Social Media Fact Sheet. www.pewresearch.org/ internet/fact-sheet/social-media/.

Pieterse, A. L., Todd, N. R., Neville, H. A., & Carter, R. T. (2012). Perceived racism and mental health among Black American adults: A meta-analytic review. *Journal of Counseling Psychology, 59*, 1–9. https://doi.org/10.1037/ a0026208.

Pluta, A., Mazurek, J., Wojciechowski, J., et al. (2023). Exposure to hate speech deteriorates neurocognitive mechanisms of the ability to understand others' pain. *Scientific Reports, 13*, 4127. https://doi.org/10.1038/S41598-023-31146-1.

Pratto, F., Sidanius, J., Stallworth, L., & Malle, B. (1994). Social dominance orientation: A personality variable predicting social and political attitudes. *Journal of Personality and Social Psychology, 67*, 741–763. https://doi.org/ 10.1037/0022-3514.67.4.741.

Priesemuth, M., & Schminke, M. (2024). Toxic work climates: An integrative review and development of a new construct and theoretical framework. *Journal of Applied Psychology.* https://doi.org/10.1037/apl0001188.

Pyszczynski, T., Abdollahi, A., Solomon, S., et al. (2006). Mortality salience, martyrdom, and military might: The Great Satan versus the Axis of Evil. *Personality and Social Psychology Bulletin, 32*, 525–537. https://doi.org/ 10.1177/0146167205282157.

Quillian, L. (1995). Prejudice as a response to perceived group threat: Population composition and anti-immigrant and racial prejudice in Europe. *American Sociological Review, 60*, 586–611. https://doi.org/10.2307/ 2096296.

Racial and Religious Hatred Act of 2006, United Kingdom (2006). www .legislation.gov.uk/ukpga/2006/1.

Ragland, K. P., & Sommers, S. A. (2024). Can I see myself there? How Black potential applicants use diversity cues to learn about graduate program culture. *Journal of Experimental Psychology: General.* https://doi.org/ 10.1037/xge0001571.

Rattan, A., & Dweck, C. S. (2010). Who confronts prejudice? The role of implicit theories in the motivation to confront prejudice. *Psychological Science, 21*, 952–959. https://doi.org/10.1177/0956797610374740.

Reyna, C., Bellovary, A., & Harris, K. (2022). The psychology of White nationalism: Ambivalence toward a changing America. *Social Issues and Policy Review, 16*, 79–124. https://doi.org/10.1111/sipr.12081.

Rice, D. R., Abrams, D., Badea, C., et al. (2010). What did you just call me? European and American ratings of the valence of ethnophaulisms. *Journal of Language and Social Psychology, 29*, 117–131. https://doi.org/10.1177/0261927X09351696.

Riek, B. M., Mania, E. W., & Gaertner, S. L. (2006). Intergroup threat and outgroup attitudes: A meta-analytic review. *Personality and Social Psychology Review, 10*, 336–353. https://doi.org/10.1207.s15327957pspr1004_4.

Rosette, A. S., Carton, A. M., Bowes-Sperry, L., & Hewlin, P. F. (2013). Why do racial slurs remain prevalent in the workplace? Integrating theory on inter-group behavior. *Organization Science, 24*, 1402–1421. https://doi.org/10.1287/orsc.1120.0809.

Rothbart, M., & Park, B. (1986). On the confirmability and disconfirmability of trait concepts. *Journal of Personality and Social Psychology, 50*, 131–142. https://doi.org/10.1037/0022-3514.50.1.131.

Roussos, G., & Dovidio, J. F. (2018). Hate speech is in the eye of the beholder: The influence of racial attitudes and freedom of speech beliefs on perceptions of racially motivated threats of violence. *Social Psychological and Personality Science, 9*, 176–185. https://doi.org/10.117/1948550617748728.

Roussos, G., & Dovidio, J. F. (2019). Enhancing the salience of free speech rights increases differential perceived free speech protections for criminal acts against Black versus White targets. *Journal of Applied Social Psychology, 49*, 519–533. https://doi.org/10.1111/JAPS.12601.

Rubino, C., Avery, D. R., McKay, P. F., et al. (2018). And justice for all: How organizational justice climate deters sexual harassment. *Personnel Psychology, 71*, 519–544. https://doi.org/10.1111/peps.12274.

Ruscher, J. B. (2001). *Prejudiced communication*. New York: Guilford Press.

Saleh, H., Alhothali, A., & Moria, K. (2023). Detection of hate speech using BERT and hate speech word embedding with deep model. *Applied Artificial Intelligence, 37*, e216671910. https://doi.org/1080.08839514.2023.2166719.

Santos, F. P., Lelkes, Y., & Levin, S. A. (2021). Link recommendation algo-rithms and dynamics of polarization in online social networks. *Proceedings of the National Academy of Sciences, 118*, e2102141118. https://doi.org/10.1073/pnas.2102141118.

Sarrasin, O., Green, E. G. T., Fasel, N., et al. (2012). Opposition to antiracism laws across Swiss municipalities: A multi-level analysis. *Political Psychology, 33*, 659–681. https://doi.org/1.1111/j.1467-9221.2012.00895.x.

Schaeffer, K., & Edwards, K. (2022). Black Americans differ from other U.S. adults over whether individual or structural racism is a bigger problem. *Pew Research Center.* https://pewrsr.ch/3EvOYgv.

Schell, C. J., Dyson, K., Fuentes, T. L., et al. (2020). The ecological and evolutionary consequences of systemic racism in urban environments. *Science, 369*(6510). https://doi.org/10.1126/science.aay4497.

Schmuck, D., & Matthes, J. (2017). Effects of economic and symbolic threat appeals in right-wing populist advertising on anti-immigrant attitudes: The impact of textual and visual appeals. *Political Communication, 34*, 607–626. https://doi.org/10.1080/10584609.2017.1316807.

Schnake, S. B., & Ruscher, J. B. (1998). Modern racism as a predictor of the linguistic intergroup bias. *Journal of Language and Social Psychology, 17*, 486–493. https://doi.org/10.1177/0261927x980174004.

Schneider, K. T., Hitlan, R. T., & Radhakrishnan, P. (2000). An examination of the nature and correlates of ethnic harassment experiences in multiple contexts. *Journal of Applied Psychology, 85*, 3–12. https://doi.org/10.1037/0021-9010.85.1.3.

Select Committee to Investigate the January 6th Attack on the U.S. Capitol (June 1, 2022). *Interview of Wandrea Arshaye Moss.* www.fox5atlanta.com/news/jan-6th-committee-releases-full-testimony-of-fulton-county-election-workers).

Sharrow, E. A., Tarsi, M. R., & Nteta, T. M. (2021). What's in a name? Symbolic racism, public opinion, and the controversy over the NFL's Washington football team name. *Race and Social Problems, 13*, 110–121. https://doi.org/10.1007/s12552-020-09305-0.

Shen, W., Lam, J., Varty, C. T., Krstic, A., & Hideg, I. (2024). Diversity climate affords unequal protection against incivility among Asian workers: The COVID-19 pandemic as a racial mega-threat. *Applied Psychology, 73*, 34–56. https://doi.org/10.1111/apps.12462.

Simon, L., & Greenberg, J. (1996). Further progress in understanding the effects of derogatory ethnic labels: The role of preexisting attitudes toward the targeted group. *Personality and Social Psychology Bulletin, 22*, 1195–1204. https://doi.org/10.1177/01461672962212001.

Simonton, T. (2018). U. of Washington Settles Campus Republications' Free Speech Lawsuit for $127,000. www.chronicle.com/article/U-of-Washington-Settles/243704.

Sittenthaler, S., Steindl, C., & Jonas, E. (2015). Legitimate vs. illegitimate restrictions – A motivational and physiological approach investigating reactance processes. *Frontiers in Psychology, 6,* 632. https://doi.org/10.3389/fpsyg.2015.00632.

Smith, L. G. E., & Postmes, T. (2011). The power of talk: Developing discriminatory group norms through discussion. *British Journal of Social Psychology, 50,* 193–215. https://doi.org/10.1348/014466610x504805.

Sohoni, D., & Sohoni, T. W. (2014). Perceptions of immigrant criminality: Crime and social boundaries. *The Sociological Quarterly, 55,* 49–71. https://doi.org/10.1111/tsq.12039.

Soral, W., Bilewicz, M., & Winiewski, M. (2018). Exposure to hate speech increases prejudice through desensitization. *Aggressive Behavior, 77,* 136–146. https://doi.org/10.1002/ab.21737.

Soral, W., Malinowska, K., & Bilewicz, M. (2022). The role of empathy in reducing hate speech proliferation: Two contact-based interventions in online and off-line settings. *Peace and Conflict: Journal of Peace Psychology, 28,* 361–371. https://doi.org/10.1037/pac0000602.

Spender, D. (1980). *Man made language.* London: Routledge & Kegan Paul.

Stanford, K. L. (2011). Keepin' it real in hip hop politics: A political perspective of Tupac Shakur. *Journal of Black Studies, 42,* 3–22. https://doi.org/10.1177/0021934709355122.

Stanley, J. (1973). Paradigmatic Woman: The Prostitute. Presented at the South Atlantic Modern Language Association.

Stephan, W. G., & Stephan, C. W. (2000). An integrated threat theory of prejudice. In S. Oskamp (Ed.), *Reducing prejudice and discrimination* (pp. 23–45). Mahwah, NJ: Lawrence Erlbaum.

Stephan, W. G., Ybarra, O., & Rios, K. (2015). Intergroup threat theory. In T. D. Nelson (Ed.), *Handbook of prejudice, stereotyping, and discrimination* (2nd ed., pp. 255–278). Mahwah, NJ: Lawrence Erlbaum.

Sue, D. W., Alsaidi, S., Awad, M. N., et al. (2019). Disarming racial microaggressions: Microintervention strategies for targets, white allies, and bystanders. *American Psychologist, 74,* 128–142. https://doi.org/10.1037/amp0000296.

Swim, J., & Hyers, L. L. (1999). Excuse me-what did you just say?!: Women's public and responses to sexist remarks. *Journal of Experimental Social Psychology, 35,* 68–88. https://doi.org/10.1006/jesp.1998.1370.

Szymanski, D. M., & Lewis, J. A. (2015). Race-related stress and racial identity as predictors of African American activism. *Journal of Black Psychology, 41,* 170–191. https://doi.org/10.1177/0095798414520707.

Szymanski, D. M., Mikorski, R., & Dunn, T. L. (2019). Predictors of sexual minority men's sexual objectification of other men. *Journal of Social and Personal Relationships, 36*, 3631–3650. https://doi.org/10.1177/0265407519832669.

Tajfel, H., & Turner, J. C. (1986). The social identity theory of intergroup behavior. In S. Worchel & W. G. Austin (Eds.), *Psychology of intergroup relations* (pp. 7–24). Chicago, IL: Nelson-Hall.

Thomas, E. F., Amiot, C. E., Louis, W. R., & Goddard, A. (2017). Collective self-determination: How the agent of help promotes pride, well-being, and support for intergroup helping. *Personality and Social Psychology Bulletin, 43*, 662–677. https://doi.org/10.1177/0146167217695553.

Thompson, A. I., & Busby, E. C. (2023). Defending the dog whistle: The role of justifications in racial messaging. *Political Behavior, 45*, 1241–1262. https://doi.org/10.1007/s11109-021-09759-x.

Tileagă, C.(2007). Ideologies of moral exclusion: A critical discursive reframing of depersonalization, delegitimization, and dehumanization. *British Journal of Social Psychology, 46*, 717–737. https://doi.org/10.1348/014466607X186894.

Tipler, C. T. (2016). *They're sucking the system dry: Mediators and moderators of the relationship between dehumanizing metaphors for immigrants and anti-immigrant public policy attitudes.* Unpublished doctoral dissertation, Tulane University.

Tipler, C. N., & Ruscher, J. B. (2014). Agency's role in dehumanization: Non-human metaphors of outgroups. *Social and Personality Psychology Compass, 8*, 214–228. https://doi.org/10.1111/spc3.12100.

Tipler, C. N., & Ruscher, J. B. (2019). Dehumanizing representations of women: The shaping of hostile sexist attitudes through animalistic metaphors. *Journal of Gender Studies, 28*, 109–118. https://doi.org/10.1080/09589236.2017.1411790.

Tontodimamma, A., Nissi, E., Sarra, A., & Fontanella, L. (2021). Thirty years of research into hate speech: Topics of interests and their evolution. *Scientometrics, 126*, 157–179. https://doi.org/10.1007/s11192-020-03737-6.

Turner, J. C., & Oakes, P. J. (1989). Self-categorization theory and social influence. In P. B. Paulus (Eds.), *The psychology of group influence* (pp. 233–275). Hillsdale, NJ: Erlbaum.

Turner, H. A., Shattuck, A., Finkelhor, D., & Hamby, S. (2016). Polyvictimization and youth violence exposure across contexts. *Journal of Adolescent Health, 58*, 208–214. https://doi.org/10.1016/j.jadohealth.2015.09.021.

United Nations General Assembly (1948). Universal Declaration of Human Rights. www.un.org/sites/un2.un.org/files/2021/03/udhr.pdf.

Valencia, N. (July, 2022). Mississippi Police Chief Fired after Audio of Slurs Surfaces. www.cnn.com/2022/07/23/us/mississippi-police-chief-fired/index .html.

Van Assche, J., Swart, H., Schmid, K., et al. (2023). Intergroup contact is reliably associated with reduced prejudice, even in the face of group threat and discrimination. *American Psychologist, 78*, 761–774. https://doi.org/ 10.1037/ampP0001144.

Van Noorloos, M. (2013). The politicization of hate speech bans in the twenty-first century Netherlands: Law in a changing context. *Journal of Ethnic and Migration Studies, 40*, 249–265. https://doi.org/10.1080/ 1369183x.2013.851474.

Wahlström, M., Törnberg, A., & Ekbrand, H. (2020). Dynamics of violent and dehumanizing rhetoric in far-right social media. *New Media & Society, 23*, 3290–3311. https://doi.org/10.1177/1461444820952795.

Wang, S., & Kim, K. J. (2023). Content moderation on social media: Does it matter who and why moderates hate speech? *Cyberpsychology, Behavior, and Social Networking, 26*, 527–534. https://doi.org/10.1089/cyber.2022.0158.

Weinstein, M., Jensen, M. R., & Tynes, B. M. (2021). Victimized in many ways: Online and offline bullying/harassment and perceived racial discrimination in diverse racial-ethnic minority adolescents. *Cultural Diversity and Ethnic Minority Psychology, 27*, 397–407. https://doi.org/10.1037/cdp0000436.

Wesselmann, E. D., & Kelly, J. R. (2010). Cat-calls and culpability: Investigating the frequency and functions of stranger harassment. *Sex Roles, 63*, 451–462. https://doi.org/10.1007/s11199-010-9830-2.

White, M. H., & Crandall, C. S. (2017). Freedom of racist speech: Ego and expressive threats. *Journal of Personality and Social Psychology, 113*, 413–429. https://doi.org/10.1037/PSPI0000095.

Wiggins, B. E., & Bowers, G. B. (2014). Memes as genre: A structurational analysis of the memescape. *New Media and Society, 17*, 1886–1906. https:// doi.org/10.117/1461444814535194.

Williams, B. (2005). NCAA Executive Committee Issues Guidelines for Use of Native American Mascots at Championship Events. fs.ncaa.org/Docs/ PressArchive/2005/Announcements/index.html.

Wilson, J. Z. (2014). Ambient hate: Racist graffiti and social apathy in a rural community. *The Howard Journal of Criminal Justice, 53*, 377–394. https:// doi.org/10.1111/hojo.12076.

Woods, F. A., & Ruscher, J. B. (2021a). "calling-out" vs. "calling-in" prejudice: Confrontation style affects inferred motive and expected outcomes. *British Journal of Social Psychology, 60*, 50–73. https://doi.org/10.1111/bjso.12405.

Woods, F. A., & Ruscher, J. B. (2021b). Viral sticks, virtual stones: Addressing anonymous hate speech online. *Patterns of Prejudice, 55*, 265–289. https://doi.org/10.1080/0031322X.2021.1968586.

Woods, F. A., & Ruscher, J. B. (2024). What's in a name … and for whom? How public spaces named for prejudiced individuals impact targets of prejudice. *Group Processes and Intergroup Relations, 27*, 663–688. https://doi.org/10.1177/13684302231184371.

Woolfson, P. (1991). Aspects of non-verbal accommodation to language in a bilingual Montreal hospital setting. *Journal of Linguistic Anthropology, 1*, 1055–1360. https://doi.org/10.1525/jlin.1991.1.2.178.

Wright, C., Brinklow-Vaughn, R., Johannes, K., & Rodriguez, F. (2021). Media portrayals of immigration and refugees in hard and fake news and their impact on consumer attitudes. *Howard Journal of Communications, 32*, 331–351. https://doi.org/10.1080/10646175.2020.1810180.

Wright, M. F., Wachs, S., Yanagida, T., et al. (2021). Associations between severity and attributions: Differences for public and private face-to-face and cyber victimization. *American Journal of Criminal Justice, 46*, 843–891. https://doi.org/10.1007/s12103-021-09660-7.

Wypych, M., & Bilewicz, M. (2024). Psychological toll of hate speech: The role of acculturation stress in the effects of exposure to ethnic slurs on mental health among Ukrainian immigrants in Poland. *Cultural Diversity and Ethnic Minority Psychology, 30*, 35–44. https://doi.org/10.1037/cdp0000522.

YouTube (2019). Hate speech policy. https://support.google.com/youtube/answer/2801939?hl=en&ref_topic=9282436

Zillman, D. (1999). Exemplification theory: Judging the whole by some of its parts. *Media Psychology, 1*, 69–94. https://doi.org/10.1207/s1532785xmep0101_5.

Zimmer, B. (2018). "Wop" Doesn't Mean What Andrew Cuomo Thinks It Means. *The Atlantic*. www.theatlantic.com/politics/archive/2018/04/wop-doesnt-mean-what-andrew-cuomo-thinks-it-means/558659/.